GLOW UP
GIRL

GLOW UP

GIRL

Overcoming Insecurity
From the Inside Out

Mindy Rocuant

Glow Up Girl: Overcoming Insecurity From the Inside Out by Mindy Rocuant

Published by Mindy Rocuant

Cover photo by Mike Rocuant

Cover design by Amina N. (Design_erya)

First paperback edition June 2023

I am not a therapist. This book does not replace the advice of a professional therapist or medical professional.

Paperback ISBN: 979-8-9884193-0-3
eBook ISBN: 979-8-9884193-1-0

Scripture quotations are taken from the *Holy Bible*, New Living Translation, copyright © 1996, 2004, 2007 by Tyndale House Foundation. Used by permission of Tyndale House Publishers, Inc., Carol Stream, Illinois 60188. All rights reserved.

To my husband Mike:

I dedicate this book to you. You are my best friend for life and you have shown me what God's love for me looks like. I love you.

TABLE OF CONTENTS

Introduction

Acknowledgements
Resources

INTRODUCTION

This book was born out of intense struggle. I fought some of my hardest battles while writing it. Satan made sure the journey wasn't easy, but I'll tell you what he didn't know: This book produced, alongside the struggle, an endurance that I hadn't had previously, and I can say now that it was worth every fight. Jesus was with me through it all, and I was never alone in the valley or the mountain.

This book is the story of my life. It was born through years of emotional pain, fear, and shame. But what gave me the strength to make the changes I needed to make in order to find healing was merely a dream for many years. I had to endure a waiting period, during which my character was tested, and I really didn't even know if what I was waiting for was real or not. I didn't know if my dreams of being free would ever become true. I didn't know if I would ever find healing, or if I would forever be stuck in the vicious cycle of fear.

I can tell you in no uncertain terms that *I have found the Healer of souls.* In just four short years, He has transformed my heart! Of course, he will always be working on my heart, until he takes me home. But I have found him! I want to share him with you. I want you to know him too! He is the sweetest joy, the purest love, the most beautiful one!

I had to undergo rigorous growth. I still do, and I always will. God isn't easy on you. He is kind. He is love. But he isn't here to promise you a life of ease. He is there *through* the hard. That is the beauty of God. I don't want a God who merely promises wealth and life with no heart change. This book very clearly portrays this truth.

One of my biggest pet peeves is when people sugarcoat things. If you know me, you know that I am very straightforward and usually blunt! Maybe a little too much sometimes! But I want to say that this book isn't an easy book to read. It will challenge you and maybe offend you. It will most likely trigger you. Maybe it will make you mad sometimes. But I ask you, when you feel triggered or upset, to please give it another chance. Take a break from reading, do your homework to process your feelings, and then try again. I promise, it's more than worth it!

Throughout the book, I will refer to my story to give reference points for the things I share. I grew up in a Mennonite church. While the Mennonites teach the truths about the life, death, and resurrection of Jesus, they do not have a solid grasp on the power of the Holy Spirit. Most of what I learned from them was that my identity was found in my outward appearance and that following rules was what my relationship with God consisted of.

My family originally came from British Columbia, Canada. When I was four, we moved to southern California - a big change for us. We lived in three different houses there. I was ten when we moved to Idaho. A few months later, we moved to Oregon, and a few months later, we moved to Iowa. We lived there for about three years, and then we moved back to southern California, to the same place as before. Each move was made because we were searching for a church that matched my family's desires - a Mennonite one, of course.

As a child, these moves tore my heart apart. I know that my family did the best they could, and under the circumstances it was easy for no one. But I ended up broken-hearted and confused, wondering who was right and who was wrong and with no answers except to just do what I was told. I was a good girl. I did what I was told - outwardly. Because that was what was expected of me, no one ever thought I would do anything differently. But the years of secret questioning forced me to find some answers, and I knew it had to be away from that religious environment. I moved to Sacramento, where I learned to know my mentor who taught me how to truly know and love Jesus and to obey him outside of a religious belief system. Gradually my heart found healing in a living relationship with the living God. He was so gracious as to provide me with a loving marriage and a beautiful family. My husband Mike is my favorite person in the world and our son Liam makes our lives spicy with laughter and fun and new challenges every day. Liam was three months old when we moved to Mayer, Arizona, and that is where my life finds me today.

Congratulations on finding this book in your hands! Don't be afraid to dig deep. Allow your heart to be soft. I pray that you will truly *see* and *experience* the love of Jesus through these pages.

"When I think of all this, I fall to my knees and pray to the Father, the Creator of everything in heaven and on earth. I pray that from his glorious, unlimited resources he will empower you with inner strength through his Spirit. Then Christ will make his home in your hearts as you trust in him. Your roots will grow down into God's love and keep you strong. And may you have the power to understand, as all God's people should, how wide, how long, how high, and how deep his love is. May you experience the love of Christ, though it is too great to understand fully. Then you will be made complete with all the fullness of life and power that comes from God.

"Now all glory to God, who is able, through his mighty power at work within us, to accomplish infinitely more than we might ask or think. Glory to him in the church and in Christ Jesus through all generations forever and ever! Amen."

Ephesians 3:14-21

PART 1

THE GLOW UP BLUEPRINT

CHAPTER 1

THE MAP TO THE INNER TREASURE

Insecurity often happens because an inner part of yourself is stagnant. The inside of you has the key to solving this problem. Insecurities about yourself are merely a manifestation of a heart issue. In this chapter, we will explore the foundation to learning a new way of thinking and a four-step process of uncovering the deeper beliefs and thoughts at the heart of your behavior.

The Heart of the Matter

A heart issue takes a lot of work to solve. You must be willing to take steps to grow. Your attitude towards yourself manifests in how much you are willing to grow yourself, and if you are unwilling to grow, that is a sure sign of the victim mindset, which we will talk about later. I have learned that one of the most important ways of showing love, in any relationship, even to yourself, is to grow. Love is manifested in tangible ways, while feelings are merely a by-product of the practicality of love. So, if you need to learn how to love yourself, you must grow yourself.

The good thing about growth is that it takes one step at a time. Love begins as a seed. It begins small, and it slowly takes steps forward.

Jesus said that "The Kingdom of Heaven is like a mustard seed planted in a field. It is the smallest of all seeds, but it becomes the largest of garden plants; it grows into a tree, and birds come and make nests in its branches." Matthew 13:31-32

This is the power of one small action, repeated many times over. Actions are always directional; actions take you either one way or another. Actions are not neutral. Either you act in a negative way, or you act in a positive way. One small action can set you on a course you will regret. One small action can set you up for success. Why? One small action becomes a habit. Habits are everyday behavior. Everyday behavior is the life you live.

Proverbs 4:23 says, "Guard your heart above all else, for it determines the course of your life."

Why is your heart so important?

If you try to change yourself outwardly without changing yourself inwardly, the changes will not last. You will always go in the direction of what your heart wants to do, because that is who you really are. Outward security is a result of inner hard work. That is the kind of security, coming from inside of you, that produces real beauty.

We are not naturally beautiful inside. We naturally behave in selfish ways because our hearts naturally desire to please ourselves instead of God. Sin means that in my heart, I am the one in control. I decide what I want, when I want it, and whoever stands in the way of those desires becomes the target of my anger.

This is why Jesus came to die for your heart. He did not die to save you from your outward actions. He came to die so that your heart would become his, and you would be changed from the inside out. He says, "Wherever your treasure is, there the desires of your heart will also be." Matthew 6:21

What makes you truly beautiful? What do you want more than anything else? What do you believe makes you truly beautiful? What desires, satisfied, make you happy, and what desires, unfulfilled, make you angry?

Jesus sees deeper than the mirror that reflects to you your outward appearance. There is nothing wrong with being outwardly beautiful. Every woman wants to be beautiful. It is where your heart is that matters. Nothing is less attractive than a woman with a selfish heart, trying to get attention for herself. True beauty is found in a woman who genuinely loves Jesus and desires him to be at the center of her heart.

Jesus is where true growth happens. He will stretch you. If you allow your insecurities about yourself to keep you inside your safety bubble, you will not become secure. You must be willing to grow, which means you must tell your comfort zone goodbye. You must want to grow more than you want to stay safe. Ironically, staying safe is dangerous. Safety is where insecurities thrive; growth is where security becomes real.

Proverbs 31:30 says, "Charm is deceptive, and beauty does not last; but a woman who fears the Lord will be greatly praised."

A woman who cherishes the Lord's desires above her own is willing to obey him, no matter the cost. A woman who is worried about people's opinions will think twice before obeying, and chances are, she will produce an excuse to not do what God wants. God searches hearts. He searches minds. He sees below your face. Your safety, your protection, it does not hide you from God. He knows what you want. He knows your heart. Growing is always a battle. Desires conflict. But the more that you choose to grow and to obey, the more you will move in a positive direction. Choices gain momentum.

God does not measure your beauty or value by how well you perform. He is not interested in your actions as much as he is interested in your heart. He is not interested in your outward appearance as much as he is interested in your heart.

There is an inner beauty that is more beautiful than outward beauty. When the inside of a woman is fully illuminated, she will shine out against the darkness with radiance. It is a heavenly glory.

How does this beauty happen? Where does it come from?

It happens by death.

Those selfish desires to be at the center, to stay safe, to protect yourself, those desires must die. The desires of your heart that conflict with God, the desires of your heart that put you on the throne, those desires must die.

On the inside, you and I need to die so that Jesus can shine in his beauty. He is more beautiful than anything else. Only he is worthy of that center position of your heart. His beauty lasts. He can transform you into a beautiful, secure person when you let him transform your heart.

Understanding the Inner You

Living in insecurity about yourself and feeling as though you never measure up shuts down your inner self. You have another side to yourself that knows the truth.

One time when I was struggling with self-hatred and anxiety about myself, I was talking to God about it. His voice spoke to me so clearly, I could not miss it. He said that I have this other side to myself that is a fighter, and that I am not all bad. (He called me a fighter because when I struggle with self-hatred, I tend to not fight.) I received a new view of myself at that moment. This is why you face inner struggles. The selfish side of you desires to be seen and heard, but when you give in to those desires, the side of you that knows better is awakened, and there is a battle over your heart. Whichever side you pay attention to is the side that wins.

Your inner self wants to be secure. It wants to be beautiful on the inside. It wants to be bold, and open, and go out of its shell. You are the only one, with the power of the Holy Spirit, who can let it out. You are the only one, along with Jesus, who has the power to set it free. This is the "you" that Jesus died to liberate. While the new self comes to life, the old self will die.

Insecurity is the voice that tells you, "You're not good enough. I don't know what God was thinking when he made you, but he sure messed up!"

"God did a good job on *her,* but he did a bad job on you."

"Your voice is weird. Why do you sound so stupid? I bet everyone notices it, except you."

"I can't believe you made such a dumb mistake! No one else has ever been so stupid!"

There is the side of you that fully believes the lies. You internalize them. You begin to repeat them to yourself. But when you allow Jesus to come in, He lets loose your other side. He gives life to the part of you that loves him.

No one else can release you from the prison of lies, except yourself with the power of Jesus. You have a side of yourself that is strong enough to push back. Jesus gives you freedom, but you must learn how to exercise your muscles and fight. He will not do all the work for you.

It is a miracle.

There is a four-step process that will help you discover your inner life.

#1 Reveal

If you have chosen to live in a safety bubble, you need to become honest to pop the bubble. A lie will only live in darkness. Exposure kills lies.

The exposure process is gut-wrenching. Realizing the full extent and impact that lies have had on you is shocking. But the pain will become healed as you become honest and learn to open up more.

Becoming honest with yourself takes a lot of courage. It takes guts to admit that you have not been living the truth. It takes strength to face your fears and to listen to a new voice. Usually, fear is one of the biggest hindrances to honesty. But trust me, fear is full of air. It really has nothing on you. Do not look at it. Look at Jesus. He already knows the truth about you anyway.

This process begins with asking yourself tough questions - and giving real answers.

- What am I telling myself about myself?
- Why am I telling myself that?
- When did I start to tell myself that?
- Was it spoken to me or over me by someone else?
- What do I feel about myself?
- What am I afraid of?
- What am I angry about?

A lie that you have internalized becomes true to you, because you believe it and repeat it to yourself over and over. But just because you have believed it does not make it true. A lie can be attached to a circumstance, to a person (especially someone who hurt you), to an action done either by yourself or someone else, to a broken dream.

Ask God to show you the answers to the questions. He knows you better than you know yourself. Have the humility to let him reveal the truth to you.

#2 Release

A lie has authority and power only as long as you give it permission to exist in your head. But once you know that a lie is there, it is time to go to war with it. To take back authority that you previously gave to the lie, you need to know what kind of weapons you have and how to use them.

Paul says in 2 Corinthians 10:3-5, "We are human, but we don't wage war as humans do. We use God's mighty weapons, not worldly weapons, to knock down the strongholds of human reasoning and to destroy false arguments. We destroy every proud obstacle that keeps people from knowing God. We capture their rebellious thoughts and teach them to obey Christ."

This is an unseen battle, fought against unseen powers and strongholds. It takes a spiritual understanding to wage the weapons of God. The thing that makes it the trickiest is that it is inside of you, and you can deceive yourself with human reasoning, false arguments, proud obstacles, and rebellious thoughts. This is why you need God's wisdom and not your own to fight the battles in your mind.

In Ephesians 6, Paul lists the armor that God makes available to us: the belt of truth, the body armor of God's righteousness, the shoes of peace, the shield of faith, the helmet of salvation, and the sword of the Spirit, the Word of God. (v. 14-17)

If you look closely, you realize that only one of these pieces of armor is a weapon. Truth, righteousness, peace, faith, and salvation are all shown here as protection. What you use to fight is the Word of God, the Sword of the Spirit.

Hebrews 4:12-13 says, "For the word of God is alive and powerful. It is sharper than the sharpest two-edged sword, cutting between soul and spirit, between joint and marrow. It exposes our innermost thoughts and desires. Nothing in all creation is hidden from God. Everything is naked and exposed before his eyes, and he is the one to whom we are accountable."

Where we can be so easily blinded by our own desires and captured by our own thoughts, God's word exposes our "innermost thoughts and desires." His word is potent, designed to cut off the enemy and to give us revelation. His word is alive because it is attached to his Holy Spirit. If you need to have his word come alive to you, you need to have a revelation of the Holy Spirit. He will reveal to you what you need to know. It is not only about the *written* word; it is also about the *spoken* word. He is still speaking today the same things he moved men to write in his word. We need to have the ears to hear what he is saying. Satan knows the power of God's written and spoken word. This is why he uses lies to capture your mind and blind your spiritual perception.

God is still speaking over you and me today what he spoke to David thousands of years ago: "O Lord, you have examined my heart and know everything about me." (Psalm 139:1) He is still moving and speaking, because his Spirit is still alive.

Once you know what the lie is that you have been believing, you can find the Scripture verses that are the opposite of the lie. Then you can put those verses to work! If Satan has taken the liberty to tell you a lie, the only right response is to tell him the truth. Speak the truth out loud. Again, the power of the spoken word is tremendous. Say out loud specifically what the lie is that you need to defeat. God is giving you authority in Jesus' name over the enemy. The lie is the tool of the enemy. So clarify the lie out loud, and break its power over you in Jesus' name. That is authority.

#3 Replace

Now, you are at the place in your spirit of standing face to face with the enemy, Satan, the father of lies. You are holding the Sword of the Spirit against his neck. But that is not enough. You need to take that sword of the living Word and plunge it into his heart. When you do that, Satan loses his power and hold on you. His lies must leave.

This next step will help you to wield that sword like a true warrior.

You've spoken out the lie, you've broken its power. You've claimed the blood of Jesus and spoken out the truth. When you have done this, you will feel a shift. Satan doesn't like the truth, and he won't leave unless you continue to stand your ground until he does leave. Don't back down. You are not his victim.

When the lies are gone, your work is only beginning. This is where growth begins!

If the lies are not replaced with thoughts of truth, the vacancy will most definitely be overrun with lies all over again. Use that sword. Use it to its fullest advantage. It is alive because the Spirit is its owner. He gives you full access to it, to himself. Take those words and begin to use them for your battle strategy.

Spoken words have power, especially God's word. Speak God's words over yourself, in every place where there has been a lie. The lies will try to come back. Know your weak points. Know where your heart is triggered. Those are the best places to cover in prayer and the word of the Lord.

#4 Restore

#1 Reveal the lie.
#2 Release the lie.
#3 Replace with truth.

These steps will need to be continuously repeated for the rest of your life. You are a warrior. Your mind is a battleground, and neither side will rest until eternity.

The fourth step is forgiveness.

God is clear that forgiveness defines your relationship with him. Jesus says in Matthew 6:14-15, "If you forgive those who sin against you, your heavenly Father will forgive you. But if you refuse to forgive others, your Father will not forgive your sins."

No matter who you are, someone has hurt you at some point. What you do with this pain can be the defining point of your life. When someone in your life has caused you pain, one of Satan's favorite strategies is to take that pain and twist it into a lie. But now that you can identify the lies, you have the power from the Holy Spirit to change your response. Rather than holding onto pain and giving yourself an excuse to stay inside of your safety bubble, you now can seize the Sword of the Spirit, pop the bubble, and release yourself from prison.

Satan doesn't want you to know that you aren't a victim.

You are not a victim. You are more than victorious.

Forgiveness has a lot to do with personal responsibility. If you want to move forward and step out of your comfort zone, there's a lot of responsibility waiting for you. Being more than victorious sounds glamorous, but you cannot be more than victorious if you don't put in the work. Jesus has done his part to make you more than a victor. Now, it is your part.

You are more than victorious. You are a daughter of God.

Exercises

#1 Reveal

What am I feeling right now?

Why am I feeling this way?

What lies am I believing?

Where do the lies come from?

What am I allowing to control my mind?

What shuts me down?

What causes me to stop dreaming?

What is my biggest fear?

#2 Release

This step is all about creating awareness. When you have lived for a long time with habits of thinking a certain way, it requires a commitment to daily train yourself to think differently-not an easy task. Catch yourself in the act of believing a lie. Don't let the lie go. It's easy to slip, especially in the beginning. The beginning is the hardest.

Find the Scripture verses that speak to the lies in your head. I have often turned on audio Scriptures when Satan was fighting to shut my mouth. Not today, Satan!

Speak those verses out loud. The louder, the better. I remember many car drives when I would use the time to really get the words out with volume. Spoken words shift the atmosphere drastically. Satan hears what you say. Say it as though you believe it! Take authority over your mind.

Journal section:

Bible verses:

#3 Replace

Once you have become honest about your struggles, and you are working to create awareness where you need to change your belief systems, you need to replace the lies with the truth.

This is a constant process. Your brain has literal grooves in it from thinking the same way for so long. It takes time and repetition to change it, to create new grooves. This is where the bigger tests happen.

Replacing the lies with the truth happens when you constantly, with awareness and intention, tell yourself something different. It won't happen by accident. It won't happen by itself. It takes work. Especially when you are struggling with a lie, that is when you need to tell yourself the truth.

Journal section:

The Map to the Inner Treasure

#4 Forgive

Forgiveness is often pure choice. It rarely has anything to do with feelings. In fact, you may still feel anger and hatred. But in the middle of feeling angry and hateful, the choice to forgive has the power to break those chains. Only Jesus has the power to help you to choose forgiveness through heated emotions.

Journal section:

Who do I need to forgive?

For what do I need to forgive?

CHAPTER 2

HOW TO OVERCOME SELF-HATRED: THE POWER OF AGREEMENT

Identity is very personal. Identity is shaped by the people and circumstances in your life. It is shaped by what you do with the people and circumstances in your life. Your heart response to difficulties will determine whether your identity becomes twisted away from God or aligned with God. It is extremely powerful and liberating when you begin to understand who you are, but when your perception of yourself is less than who you want to be, it is very limiting.

Ephesians 2:10 says that God made you to do good things, and that he planned those good things in advance. Before you were even born, God had a plan for your life. But what if you were told that you'll never measure up? That you don't have what it takes? What if you perceive yourself to be a disappointment? What if you believe that you are unable to do a good job at something new? What if the dreams that you had for yourself were too big or didn't fit someone else's plan for you?

Not only do you question who you are, but you begin to believe you'll never be who you really wanted to be.

I don't know your story. But I do know mine. I have gone from wholeheartedly believing that I would never be good enough, to stumbling through the process of unlearning that belief system, to replacing that belief with the truth that I am strong enough to be the person who God made me to be. Yes, I have bad days when I struggle to fill my mind with truth, but I have come a very long way. I truly believe that anyone can learn to overcome the blocks that hinder them.

The Battle of Worship

Romans 12:1-2 says, "And so, dear brothers and sisters, I plead with you to give your bodies to God because of all he has done for you. Let them be a living and holy sacrifice - the kind he will find acceptable. This is truly the way to worship him. Don't copy the behavior and customs of this world, but let God transform you into a new person by changing the way you think. Then you will learn to know God's will for you, which is good and pleasing and perfect."

These verses are showing us the battle that is being fought in your mind for your identity every day. It is fought on many levels and from many angles. Satan wants to hide your identity from you, so he uses the weak areas in your thinking to slip lies into your mind. His biggest lies are where you fight your hardest battles, and where you fight your hardest battles is where your true self is, who you are designed to be.

Your greatest struggle in life is destined to be your greatest victory. If you need to know who you are, look at your life and find where you fight your hardest and strongest battles (in your mind). For some of us, it's where we have given up. Where you have lost hope and allowed yourself to shut down. Or it may be a stronghold of fear. Maybe fear was the reason you gave up.

Here are some great questions to ask yourself:

- Where is my area(s) of greatest struggle?
- Where do I find myself constantly fighting a battle?

- Where have I given up?
- Where have I lost hope?
- Where have I allowed myself to shut down?
- Where have I stopped dreaming?
- What am I afraid of?

The honest answers to these questions will give you clues to search your heart and truly discover who you are made to be.

Another way to figure out who you really are is to examine your life and ask yourself what you need every day.

- If you are obsessed with health
- If you need to be affirmed by your friends
- If you must perform well in your job or school

Etc.

Of course, health, affirmation, or success is not a bad thing. It is the need that drives it. The need exposes an area of insecurity, where you are clinging to an outward source for safety. The need is also surrounded by lies, such as "If I am not a certain weight, I am ugly." or "If my friends don't like me, I'm not likable." or "If I don't do this much work, I'm a bad worker." Your security is dependent on the scale, friends, and work. Pretty shaky, sad security, shattered as soon as the weight goes up or new friends arrive, or your score goes down at work.

Some more great questions to ask yourself:

- What do I think that I need in order to feel safe?
- Why do I need it?
- How does my need drive my behavior?

Matthew 6:33 says, "Seek the kingdom of God above all else, and live righteously, and he will give you everything you need."

Finding your identity in an outward source will always fail you, and you will end up more broken than you were before. But if you consider God to be more important to you than anything else, you will have everything you need in him to feel safe and secure. Satan uses good things like health, love, and success to make you think that unless you are at a certain place in health, love, or success (or anything else), that you've failed as a person. He makes you think that your value comes from your performance.

On the other side, God is fighting for you. He has a plan for you, and he never gives up on you.z

There is a central part of you that both sides are after. This central part of you is not neutral. It is either being swayed by the lies of the enemy, or it is being intentionally filled with truth, by you. There is no middle ground here. In this fight, you need to know your weak points and to know how to resist the enemy.

The central part of you was stolen by Satan, way back in the garden of Eden, when he asked Eve, "Did God really say?..." (Genesis 3:1) The moment Eve chose to question God's word, sin was planted in her heart. The desire for control took over. The desire to be wise became more important than to be connected to the source of wisdom, her Creator.

The central battle in this central part of you is worship.

Worship is not only singing songs in church on Sunday. It is a lifestyle. But more than that, it is the heart of why you do what you do. It is what defines how you choose to live. It is beneath every struggle. It is the battle of battles, and who you choose to worship (self or God) is who will win the battle.

Some great questions to ask yourself:

- How quickly do I respond to God's voice?
- Do I tend to question him?
- Dismiss him?
- Or do I immediately listen and then do what he says?

- What does my heart look like?
- Am I filling my heart with truth or am I allowing any thought to come in?

How quickly you choose to either dismiss or respond to God's voice will show you how little or how much of your heart he has access to.

There is hope.

God knows that without him, there is no way for you to win the battle. The battle is lost the moment you choose to believe that you don't need him.

God has given you tools to use in this fight, to take back the ground the enemy stole from you. You're not hopeless, helpless, or lost.

We think that we know better than God what we need, and we get mad at him when he doesn't do what we want.

But that's worship of myself.

Worship of God is obedience.

Worship of God is agreeing with his Spirit.

Romans 8:15-16 says," So you have not received a spirit that makes you fearful slaves. Instead, you received God's Spirit when he adopted you as his own children. Now we call him, 'Abba, Father.' For his Spirit joins with our spirit to affirm that we are God's children."

You and I are God's daughters. God is our Father.

Even when Satan stole humanity by causing Eve to question God, Eve was still God's daughter. God never changed.

Even now, when you're not sure who you are and you're questioning God, you're still God's daughter. God still hasn't changed.

Satan, on the other hand, is the father of lies and he will target you with any lies or half-truths that he can. He is the one who administers a spirit of fear. He is the one who condemns and blames. He will never let you forgive yourself for your mistakes and sin.

Essentially, *Satan is the minister of self-hatred.*

What is self-hatred?

Self-hatred is one of the tools Satan uses to cripple you. He uses it to limit you.

Self-hatred is the fruit of a "less-than" belief system.

It is full of unbelief. It means that you don't believe what God says about you.

It is full of pride. It causes you to think too much about yourself.

It is full of jealousy. It creates discontentment in your heart about yourself and causes you to compare yourself to others.

It causes confusion, clamor, and noise in your head. It distracts you from your purpose. When God tries to speak to you, you already disqualify yourself from obeying him, because you don't believe he loves you.

Self-hatred takes you to a dark place. It's low. It's mean. It gives you abusive thoughts towards yourself.

I believe it is time to show self-hatred to the door.

30

You are strong enough to kick it out. You are God's daughter.

Agreeing with God

You may be asking, how do I actually kick self-hatred out of my heart?

In chapter 1, we went over the map to the heart:

Reveal (be honest)

Release (bind lies)

Replace (speak truth)

Restore (forgive)

My path to victory over self-hatred was exactly that. It started with getting honest about how I really felt about myself. I was surprised to realize how intensely I hated myself. I told myself all kinds of lies about myself. I had to develop awareness about my self-talk. I then had to learn what God said about me and put his words in the place of the lies. Self-hatred was a hard and long battle for me. I fought it every day for months, probably even years. I still fight it sometimes. But self-hatred is a demon and a lie who knows who I really am, and all I need to do is to remind it who I am in Christ, and it must leave.

The beautiful part of it is that once you begin to have victory, you will learn how to live a different way. Your heart will begin to rest, and you will no longer be consumed with doubting yourself and fearing the worst. Your chains will be broken off and you will live in freedom! Your identity will become solidly rooted in Jesus and what he says about you. Those good things he planned for you will come true.

Often when Jesus was performing miracles, he praised those who expressed strong faith in him. There was one time when he was visiting his home village, and his audience's lack of faith hindered his healing power. (Matthew 13:57-58)

Ephesians 2:19-21 says, "I also pray that you will understand the incredible greatness of God's power for us who believe him. This is the same mighty power that raised Christ from the dead and seated him in the place of honor at God's right hand in the heavenly realms. Now he is far above any ruler or authority or power or leader or anything else - not only in this world but also in the world to come."

This verse in Ephesians 2 says that God's incredible power is for us who believe him. I want to be like the woman who, with a history of twelve years of bleeding and being unclean, was so desperate to be free that she risked complete humiliation and possibly even death to reach out and touch the fringe of Jesus' robe. Her complete faith granted her healing and deliverance, not only from her bleeding, but also freedom from shame and fear. She knew Jesus. She had been called dirty and unclean for a lifetime, but Jesus renamed her "Daughter."

That is the kind of faith we need, faith the size of a mustard seed, but that can move mountains. This kind of faith unlocks prison doors. Faith in a God of unlimited power, who can do anything, who can change your heart.

Self-hatred starts with a questioning doubt: "Did God *really* say?"... and the lies have an open door to enter your mind. Security comes from faith, which declares that God most definitely does say what he says. Faith in God's spoken and written words opens up power to break chains, brings down walls, and crushes demonic lies.

You are always believing something. You are either believing a lie or you are believing the truth.

Agreement with a lie will grow doubt and insecurity. Agreement with truth will grow confidence and faith.

You can't trash yourself and expect yourself to shine.

You can't trash yourself and glorify God.

You can't trash yourself and be more than victorious.

But even though you may have trashed yourself, you are still God's daughter. He says you can be more than victorious.

When you understand who you are as a daughter of God, you will no longer agree with lies about yourself. You will agree with truth. Your life will begin to shine with God's glory.

This is the power of agreement. This is the power of faith. This is the power of God.

You will no longer live from a place of need. You will trust God to give you everything you need. He is everything you need. Do not try to pursue love for yourself. Pursue God. He is Love. When he is in the right place in your heart, he will fill your heart with love for yourself.

Mark 12:30-31 says, "And you must love the Lord your God with all your heart, all your soul, all your mind, and all your strength. The second is equally important: 'Love your neighbor as yourself.' No other commandment is greater than these."

You cannot love God well until you see yourself as he sees you. He is your Creator, and if you disagree with him about how he made you, that creates a disruption in your connection with him.

You cannot love others well until you see yourself as God sees you. Self-hatred forces you to compare yourself to others. Either you think you are less than others, or you think you are better, and your actions and words are shaped by these belief systems.

Loving God first is the true cure for self-hatred. It takes the focus from yourself and places it on Jesus. He is the one who names you daughter. He is the Love that every single one of us is searching for. It's only when we allow ourselves to be completely captivated by him that true change is found.

John 15:10 says, "When you obey my commandments, you remain in my love, just as I obey my Father's commandments and remain in his love."

Obedience used to be a scary thing to me, because I saw God as a big, distant Father up in the sky, ready to cut me off as soon as I slightly messed up. But as my view of God shifted, I learned that he is the kindest, most gentle and loving person in my life. That kind of perspective made me realize that I wanted to obey him! I wanted to please a God who was present and real. I wanted to be with a God who wanted me first.

God is glorified and loved by your agreement with him. The agreements with his word produce the actions of obedience that you need to take. The actions you take follow an inner agreement with God.

God made you for more than yourself. He made you to live for him. The end goal isn't to be secure because you are beautiful or successful. The end goal is to allow God to fill your heart and out of that place of abundance and agreement, you will live at rest with yourself and others.

God is not passive, and he doesn't want you to be passive either. He will stretch you. He will take you out of your comfort zone. He wants you to be comfortable with who you are, but for you to be comfortable with who you are, he knows that you must be stretched and grown. Being comfortable with who you are doesn't happen in your comfort zone! It happens in your uncomfortable zone.

When you begin to make agreements with God, he'll often show you a part of yourself that needs to be changed. For me, this often triggered my insecurities all over again. I thought that if I still needed to change, I wasn't good enough yet! (Um, hello, self-hatred?!)

All that God is doing is showing you that you are exactly where you are supposed to be! A need to grow does not mean that you are less than; it means that you are a human being and that God's love is revealing to you ways to become like himself. He is showing you steps of obedience to take.

If you find yourself beginning to agree with lies again, you need to do your homework again, to bind the lies and declare the truth. Then you go to that area of yourself that needs to be changed and learn how to change yourself.

If there is a gap between who you are and who you want to be, then learn to figure out what you need to do to bridge that gap. Make yourself uncomfortable. This is where you'll fight those difficult battles over and over. This is who you are - a daughter of God, taking back the ground stolen from you by the enemy. This is who you are - a fighter. A warrior.

What do you do with other women in your life who are farther along than you, especially in your weak areas? I spent so much time worrying about this! I felt so insecure around people who were leaders, who seemed to have it together.

I learned this: Do not compare yourself to them. Your worth is not based on your level of growth. You've already agreed with God that you're worth his love for you. If he loves you, and your worth isn't a question, you have nothing to worry about.

The best thing to do is to observe those people. You can talk to them. Pick their brains and figure out what they did to get to where they are. Your battle isn't theirs, most likely. They are probably fighting a different battle than you. But people with more experience have valuable knowledge, and I place a very high value on the things I can learn from people who have gone farther than I have.

This is a time-consuming process. In fact, you will be working on this for the rest of your life! Growth doesn't happen overnight. It takes a lot of patience and grace for yourself. Self-hatred doesn't like to disappear easily, quickly, or quietly. It makes a lot of fuss, especially in the beginning. But it is the daily persistence that makes changes happen.

In the hard places of discomfort is where you are meant to sparkle. It is when you are stretched that you find life. You were made to shine. That is why God gives you opportunities to grow.

Exercises

#1 Reveal

What am I feeling right now?

Why am I feeling this way?

What lies am I believing?

Where do the lies come from?

What am I allowing to control my mind?

What shuts me down?

What causes me to stop dreaming?

What is my biggest fear?

#2 Release

This step is all about creating awareness. When you have lived for a long time with habits of thinking a certain way, it requires a commitment to daily train yourself to think differently-not an easy task. Catch yourself in the act of believing a lie. Don't let the lie go. It's easy to slip, especially in the beginning. The beginning is the hardest.

Find the Scripture verses that speak to the lies in your head. I have often turned on audio Scriptures when Satan was fighting to shut my mouth. Not today, Satan!

Speak those verses out loud. The louder, the better. I remember many car drives when I would use the time to really get the words out with volume. Spoken words shift the atmosphere drastically. Satan hears what you say. Say it as though you believe it! Take authority over your mind.

Journal section:

Bible verses:

#3 Replace

Once you have become honest about your struggles, and you are working to create awareness where you need to change your belief systems, you need to replace the lies with the truth.

This is a constant process. Your brain has literal grooves in it from thinking the same way for so long. It takes time and repetition to change it, to create new grooves. This is where the bigger tests happen.

Replacing the lies with the truth happens when you constantly, with awareness and intention, tell yourself something different. It won't happen by accident. It won't happen by itself. It takes work. Especially when you are struggling with a lie, that is when you need to tell yourself the truth.

Journal section:

#4 Forgive

Forgiveness is often pure choice. It rarely has anything to do with feelings. In fact, you may still feel anger and hatred. But in the middle of feeling angry and hateful, the choice to forgive has the power to break those chains. Only Jesus has the power to help you to choose forgiveness through heated emotions.

Journal section:

Who do I need to forgive?

For what do I need to forgive?

CHAPTER 3

HOW TO FORGIVE YOURSELF: OPENING UP THE WOUNDS

I f I haven't already triggered you, this chapter will probably do that!

Unlike a physical wound, inner hurts fester away for years, spreading bitterness and creating divisions in relationships. A heart wound is difficult to handle. Heart wounds are unseen, but very real, raw, and ugly when left alone. They manifest in many ways, and every single one of us is affected by them.

I grew up in a religious culture where pain was masked. I spent years with unresolved pain, hidden behind walls of fear, self-hatred, and shame. The religious environment taught me to push down feelings. I was afraid of being seen for who I was. I was identified as a good girl, because outwardly, I looked fine.

Although your story is probably different from mine, the point is that I can relate to hiding pain and stuffing it inside. Pretending to be okay when I was not okay at all. I lived like this for years.

The Importance of Personal Responsibility

Changing my story has taken a lot of work. I have poured myself into learning and growing. I have learned that taking personal responsibility is the key to changing myself. No one else, besides myself, can actually implement healthy habits, mindsets, and behavior patterns. No one else is responsible for my choices. I hold the key to my own healing. Yes, Jesus heals my heart, but there are a lot of practical choices that he asks me to make every single day. Even Jesus won't do all the work for me!

The same is true for you.

If a person who is perfectly healthy insists that someone needs to feed them, that person has a serious problem with laziness! But if a person who became paralyzed learns how to use their muscles, that person is seen as a miracle - and rightly so.

I think that we need to see more miracles.

The truth is that no matter who you are or where you've come from or what has happened to you, God has given you the tools to become a miracle. Glory and healing are your portion, but it only comes through trials, suffering, and pain. Any other path to glory and healing is misleading you. Instead of allowing your pain to be your excuse for not becoming a whole person, those very circumstances can be made to help you become whole, when handled correctly.

When no one and nothing is your excuse, you become unstoppable. Pain equals calling. The more you have suffered, the more you are qualified to help others who have suffered. The more closed off you were, the more potential you have to open yourself up and be a light in others' darkness.

Hebrews 4:14-16 says, "So then, since we have a great High Priest who has entered heaven, Jesus the Son of God, let us hold firmly to what we believe. This High Priest of ours understands our weaknesses, for he faced all of the same testings we do, yet he did not sin. So let us come boldly to the throne of our gracious God. There we will receive his mercy, and we will find grace to help us when we need it most."

These verses hold such great comfort. Often, in our suffering, it seems as though we are afraid to trust God with our struggles. But Jesus, who opened the door for us to heaven, faced everything we do so that he can now sympathize for us when we are weak! In John 14, the Holy Spirit is named our Helper. The very expression of God's nature is to be with us in our suffering. If that isn't comforting, I don't know what is.

Jesus has ripped back the curtain into the Holy of holies, where we can run and fall on our faces and weep into the lap of the One who has borne all our suffering. He has promised to help us.

Hebrews 5:7-9 says, "While Jesus was here on earth, he offered prayers and pleadings, with a loud cry and tears, to the one who could rescue him from death. And God heard his prayers because of his deep reverence for God. Even though Jesus was God's Son, he learned obedience from the things he suffered. In this way, God qualified him as a perfect High Priest, and he became the source of eternal salvation for all those who obey him."

Jesus laid down his right to ease. He did that for *me* and *you.* If anyone has ever been tempted to blame God for not showing up, it was Jesus. He probably wanted many times to go back to his kingly throne in heaven and have thousands and thousands of angels at his command, ready to obey him. Instead, he stayed on earth, as a servant, working with his bare hands to feed himself and dealing with complaining, entitled disciples. He didn't lose sight of the bigger picture. God was at work, doing something that required Jesus's complete sacrifice. God did not do what Jesus wanted. Jesus asked God to rescue him. But God didn't do his will; Jesus did the Father's will.

Jesus's sacrifice meant the salvation of the whole world. What does my sacrifice mean? If one soul is worth more than the whole world, I consider it more than worth it to suffer so that one soul can know Jesus.

But I have spent a lot of time blaming God for my problems. I thought my struggles were his fault. I thought he was responsible to clean up my mess.

One of the biggest lessons I've had to learn is to let God off the hook. I stayed stuck there for a long time. I complained, I argued, I fought. Finally, God told me that I needed to forgive him. I was mad at him for making me move away from people I loved. But once I forgave him, I realized that God didn't make me move. He led me to move, and I chose to obey. Losing people was the result of my choice. It was my responsibility to learn how to handle that.

The reason why the move as an adult made me so upset was that it triggered an old wound. As a child, I had to move away from my best friend. I hadn't been able to truly release that friendship, until that pain was opened again, and I had to face the same loss as an adult. As a child, I knew that I couldn't be real about how much it hurt. I had to bury the pain. As a girl, I had very few friends because I was too afraid to trust anyone.

What is a trigger?

For a wound to be healed, it must be opened up. Triggers are an essential part of the healing process. Triggers are signs pointing the way to the next step.

Triggers are unpleasant, because they reveal things that are difficult to be honest about. Triggers are current reminders of past wounds. If you do not know what to do with triggers, you will react negatively and create unhealthy behavior patterns as a result of unhealed pain.

Most of us don't like to admit we were hurt. Acknowledging pain can feel like weakness, because it makes you vulnerable. Instead, we hide the pain. It can make you feel safe and protected from future hurts, but only until something happens (aka a trigger) to remind you of that pain beneath the surface.

If you are triggered and you play the victim, you are losing the battle. You know how you react to pain, and as the days and years go by, you begin to build a thick shell by always reacting the same way.

Unhealthy reactions to triggers include:
- Suppressing memories
- Isolating yourself
- Suppressing feelings
- Refusing to talk about it
- Blaming others
- Blaming yourself
- Blaming God
- Making yourself busy
- Eating too much or not enough
- Being needy
- Hiding your needs
- Not letting yourself be alone

Maybe you have a different kind of habit built up. But each unhealthy reaction includes some way of trying to protect yourself from getting hurt again. This is completely natural. No one likes pain. However, protecting yourself is not healthy or healing.

How do you heal yourself?

In order to feel safe, you might try to control what happens to you. You don't trust yourself to open up, because you are afraid of the same old story repeating itself. So, you hold everyone off at a distance, attempting to control circumstances and relationships.

But it doesn't give you the results you're looking for. Safety is elusive, pain is ever present, and loneliness is very real. Hiding from pain doesn't make it go away. Hiding intensifies existing pain and brings on a new set of problems. You have to manage your facade, so everyone thinks you are fine. Your relationships suffer.

One of the things that happens when you build walls to protect yourself is that you begin to see yourself as the problem. You aren't thinking rationally, because you're in survival mode. Your mind takes the pain and casts you as the perpetrator. You become a prisoner of your own making.

Maybe your pain is caused by your past actions, and maybe it's not. But whether or not you are to blame, you owe it to yourself and the relationships around you to work through those problems.

In chapter 1, we covered the process of:

Reveal (be honest)
Release (bind the lies)
Replace (find the truth)
Restore (forgive)

In the restore step, I talked a little bit about forgiveness. Forgiveness is necessary to practice towards God, others, and yourself. In this chapter, I want to talk about forgiving yourself.

Forgiving Yourself

Forgiving yourself is very similar to forgiving another person. This is where the difference lies: You are a person, but the way you feel about yourself and the way you treat yourself are not as obvious as the way you feel about others and the way you treat others. The things you tell yourself are silent. The self-hatred is invisible. The hidden aspect of relating to yourself provides more layers for self-deceit.

Walls that you have built around yourself to protect yourself from pain are constructed of nothing but lies. Lies such as:

- I am worthless.
- I'll never be as good as she is.
- Nobody loves me.
- I'm all alone.
- I'm unseen.

- I'm unheard.
- No one else has ever experienced what I have.

Every single lie comes from the victim mindset. When something or someone hurts you, you react with self-protecting behavior rooted in lies. This belief system is what produces the unhealthy reactions to triggers we talked about earlier. It is my personal responsibility to examine my heart and learn what lies I am believing.

As I have been writing this chapter, Satan took those very same lies I was writing about and bombarded my mind. I know what it's like to battle self-hatred and insecurities, but this was on another level! The smallest things triggered me, and immediately, every lie I could imagine overwhelmed my brain. To make things even more chaotic and confusing, I couldn't talk. All of those thought patterns took me on a cycle deeper and deeper into self-hatred and stuck me in silence.

You see, one of the biggest lies I had always believed is that I was quiet. I had always thought my voice didn't matter. Not talking was my method to protect myself. But once I began to unpack the lies, it became apparent that my belief system (that I didn't have a voice) opened the door to a deaf and dumb demon.

Demons feed on lies and lies allowed to live in darkness will only empower demonic forces. I had to first uncover the lie (reveal), weakening the demon's power, and then I had to bind the deaf and dumb demon (release). I had to bind it in Jesus' name and command it to go away from me into hell. Then I had to invite the Holy Spirit to come and take its place (replace).

This demon used the lie that my voice didn't matter to make me not talk. Then, he muffled my spiritual ears so that I couldn't hear the truth, that my voice DOES matter.

Satan, the father of lies, knows my weak spots, and if he can get me to believe the lies, the door is opened for the deaf and dumb demon to come back. I have fought this battle many, many times. As I was saying, as I was writing this chapter, I have been targeted with lies as never before. And the lies hinder me from talking and from writing. Satan doesn't want me to share this with you. But I am exposing him, because I have been delivered from his power and I want to help you find the same freedom.

Satan will use your pain to get you to believe lies. Those lies are not accidents. They are intentionally placed for you at the exact time when you are vulnerable. During an easier season, thoughts of worthlessness don't hit the same as when you are going through something difficult. Satan knows that difficult times will happen to every single person. But if you are prepared for him, his chances of success fall. If you already know who you are, a difficult season will not take you down. It will be a testing time, a training ground, but it will not be a time of failure, unless you allow the lies in.

Healthy Responses and Forgiving Yourself

#1 Claim Your Identity

The first step to being healed and to forgiving yourself is to claim your identity as a daughter of God. You are not worthless. You belong to God. You are worth the price of his blood. If you are blaming yourself, you can claim the blood of Jesus to cleanse you. If you have been holding yourself in a cycle of lies and shame, you can relax your hold. You can let go of the version of yourself that you've been fighting to protect and discover your new self in Christ - no shame, no lies.

Romans 8:1 says, "So now there is no condemnation for those who belong to Christ Jesus."

Many of us are far harder on ourselves than we are on others. If you are already telling yourself the truth, the chances of you believing lies are much less. But no one is beyond the truth. No one is beyond Jesus.

John 14:6, "I am the way, the truth, and the life." Jesus *is* the truth.

Jesus said in John 8:31-32, "You are truly my disciples if you remain faithful to my teachings. And you will know the truth, and the truth will set you free." John 8:43, "Why can't you understand what I am saying? It's because you can't even hear me!"

The deaf and dumb demon is hindering people from knowing who they are and from hearing the truth. Because they cannot hear, they cannot understand the truth.

The truth isn't screaming for your attention. The truth is whispered to your heart in a still, small voice. You must listen for it. Satan takes advantage of your distracted moments, especially hard times, to slip lies in front of you. If you aren't trying to listen to the truth or speak the truth to yourself, the lie will seem believable. Once the lie takes root, the door is opened, and a deafness and dumbness to the truth will begin to take over.

#2 Learn How to be Vulnerable

Vulnerability takes a lot of courage. But it takes vulnerability to forgive yourself. It takes vulnerability to believe truth. If lies build walls, then truth is what takes down the walls, and that makes you vulnerable. It puts you in the place where pain could potentially happen.

But the beautiful thing about vulnerability is that it is also the place where love happens. Walls that shut out pain also shut out love. Why? Because you cannot separate love from truth. If love meant that there should be no pain, no one would be loved. I must be allowed to believe a lie if I am also allowed to choose to believe the truth.

But God is Love, and God is Truth.

Therefore, in the middle of pain, you are wholly loved. It just means that you are required to keep yourself completely open to him.

1 John 4:18 says, "[God's] love has no fear, because perfect love expels all fear. If we are afraid, it is for fear of punishment, and this shows we have not fully experienced his perfect love."

You don't need to be afraid of yourself. You don't need to be afraid of facing demons or lies or pain. God's perfect love covers you.

Romans 8:35, 37-38, says, "Does it mean he no longer loves us if we have trouble or calamity, or are persecuted, or hungry, or destitute, or in danger, or threatened with death?...No, despite all these things, overwhelming victory is ours through Christ, who loved us. And I am convinced that nothing can ever separate us from God's love."

The problem is in your mind, when you take pain to mean that God doesn't love you anymore. God's love doesn't go anywhere, but your faith in it is on shaky ground. God uses pain. He uses it for redemption. Where would growth be with no pain? Pain is not punishment. It is a lesson God uses to teach things we could not learn any other way. We must be vulnerable to it.

#3 Be Specific

Since many of us have spent years telling ourselves lies, in order to learn new self-talk, we must become aware of our old self-talk. You can't change unless you know what you need to change. You can't forgive yourself without knowing exactly what you need to forgive yourself for.

Spiritual deafness and dumbness to the truth makes everything appear fuzzy. It's difficult to articulate exactly what you feel when you can't hear or speak properly. But that is not where you are left helpless! Jesus is the truth, and his name clears away all cloudiness, confusion, and darkness. Speak his name to that deaf and dumb demon. Command it to go away, in Jesus' name. Take authority in Jesus' name over your ears and mouth, over your ability to speak and hear. Ask the Holy Spirit to speak truth to you, and to enable you to hear it.

Once all the dust clears away, lies will be exposed. Now you have the choice to be completely honest with yourself.

Honesty can quickly become ugly, because lies are ugly. But it leads to beauty, I promise! It takes a lot of hard, intentional work. But lies exposed become lies defeated. As you continue to follow the process of revealing the lies, releasing the lies, and replacing them with truth, you will learn to forgive yourself and your life will be completely changed!

This chapter is a lot to process. Take as much time as you need to go through it and evaluate your heart. Healing and forgiveness take time. My prayer and hope are that it truly helps you to release yourself and to heal yourself. Whatever your story is, there is hope, healing, and freedom for you in Christ!

As you notice how you get triggered, your reactions to the triggers, and your belief system underneath it all, it is so important to give yourself grace. There are many practical ways to learn to show kindness to yourself. Some of my favorite things to do are:

- Journaling
- Taking a bath
- Taking a walk
- Reading a good book
- Reading the Bible
- Prayer
- Playing piano
- Singing
- Going for a drive

- Getting coffee or tea
- Taking a nap
- Hanging out with godly friends
- Working out
- Joining a Bible study group

This may sound silly, but I always operate best when I drink plenty of water and eat good food. It is so basic, but so easy to overlook, and it makes a huge difference.

These things help you to stay in touch with yourself and ensure that your needs are met. Figure out what fills you up and energizes you, and then you will have what you need to love on the people in your life.

Remember to be soft in processing emotions. Feel, and feel deeply. When you start to get angry or to put up walls, that's a good indicator of hardness in your heart because of a lack of processing. Rather than trying to control and manipulate circumstances to be painless and comfortable, learn to become vulnerable to a painful season and expose yourself to love. Strength is the attitude of facing hard things and embracing pain, while being soft. Strength and softness together are the epitome of what it means for a woman to know the Lord.

Exercises

#1 Reveal

What am I feeling right now?

Why am I feeling this way?

What lies am I believing?

Where do the lies come from?

What am I allowing to control my mind?

What shuts me down?

What causes me to stop dreaming?

What is my biggest fear?

#2 Release

This step is all about creating awareness. When you have lived for a long time with habits of thinking a certain way, it requires a commitment to daily train yourself to think differently-not an easy task. Catch yourself in the act of believing a lie. Don't let the lie go. It's easy to slip, especially in the beginning. The beginning is the hardest.

Find the Scripture verses that speak to the lies in your head. I have often turned on audio Scriptures when Satan was fighting to shut my mouth. Not today, Satan!

Speak those verses out loud. The louder, the better. I remember many car drives when I would use the time to really get the words out with volume. Spoken words shift the atmosphere drastically. Satan hears what you say. Say it as though you believe it! Take authority over your mind.

Journal section:

Bible verses:

#3 Replace

-

Once you have become honest about your struggles, and you are working to create awareness where you need to change your belief systems, you need to replace the lies with the truth.

This is a constant process. Your brain has literal grooves in it from thinking the same way for so long. It takes time and repetition to change it, to create new grooves. This is where the bigger tests happen.

Replacing the lies with the truth happens when you constantly, with awareness and intention, tell yourself something different. It won't happen by accident. It won't happen by itself. It takes work. Especially when you are struggling with a lie, that is when you need to tell yourself the truth.

Journal section:

#4 Forgive

Forgiveness is often pure choice. It rarely has anything to do with feelings. In fact, you may still feel anger and hatred. But in the middle of feeling angry and hateful, the choice to forgive has the power to break those chains. Only Jesus has the power to help you to choose forgiveness through heated emotions.

Journal section:

Who do I need to forgive?

For what do I need to forgive?

PART 2
THE PRACTICAL GLOW UP

CHAPTER 4

THE TRUTH ABOUT MASCULINITY AND FEMININITY: HOW TO WORK TOGETHER

In this chapter, we will explore the dynamics of femininity and masculinity and how they are designed to relate together. This is not a marriage book. I am addressing both single and married women in this topic. These principles can and should be practiced both before and after marriage.

What does femininity mean to you? Why does it matter to you?

While you're thinking about it, I'll tell you what it means to me and why it matters to me.

Why Femininity Matters and What It Is

Femininity matters because it matters to God.

Femininity is much more than a lifestyle or a mindset. It is irreplaceable and immovable. Femininity is a mystery, and it is difficult to define; however, it is at the center of what it means to be a woman and it is essential to understand it in order to become a better woman.

Femininity is a calling on the life of every woman ever born. It is a gift, and it is the responsibility of every woman to unwrap the gift inside of herself, layer by layer. It does not matter if you do not view yourself as feminine. If you were born as a woman, you are feminine.

Femininity is a part of who you are. It is the part of your heart that lights up your womanhood. It is possible to shut down your feminine side, but it is not possible to remove it.

Femininity must be cultivated and grown. It is the fruit produced from the woman inside of you. It's like your thumbprint. It's unlike anyone else in the world. It's *you*.

Without femininity, women lack color, warmth, and life. It gives you a sense of purpose, because it's what you are created for.

Femininity matters because God created it. God called it good (Genesis 1:31). God created women to be feminine.

Femininity matters because it is part of God's character (more on that later in this chapter).

Femininity matters because wherever the prize is, that is where the fight is. And there has never been such a fight over womanhood as there is today. If femininity didn't matter, then why is there such an uproar about it? If it didn't matter, why is there such an attempt to erase it?

Femininity matters because ultimately, it's not about me. It's about *him*. It is time for women to bend their knees to worship their true King. If his design for me is to be feminine, I will choose to develop myself as a feminine woman, no matter what. It's about *him*.

What God wants matters more than what I want.

Strength and Softness: The Character Qualities of Masculinity and Femininity

I grew up thinking that men were only strong and that women were only soft. This created a lot of confusion in my mind about relationships and who I was as a woman. I have learned some surprising things in the last several years that changed my mindset entirely.

But first, let's define masculine and feminine character qualities:

- Strength is masculine.   Softness is feminine.
- Protective is masculine.   Compassion is feminine.
- Competitive is masculine. Nurturing is feminine.
- Analytical is masculine.   Creative is feminine.
- Stable is masculine.   Surrender is feminine.
- Giving is masculine.   Receiving is feminine.

If you take those feminine qualities and erase them, masculinity is no longer masculinity. What is leadership and protection with no one willing to receive leadership and protection? On the other hand, if you take masculine qualities and erase them, femininity is no longer femininity. What is compassion and nurturing with no one to nurture or have compassion on?

What does this mean? It means that whether you are a man or whether you are a woman, you need *both* masculine *and* feminine qualities.

A woman needs to be more gentle with undertones of strength.

A man needs to be more strong with undertones of gentleness.

A woman needs to be more compassionate with undertones of protection.

A man needs to be more protective with undertones of compassion.

Etc.

It is not wrong for a woman to lead, if she is not ignoring her feminine qualities and attempting to assume more of a masculine role. She must lead with kindness, gentleness, sweetness. Such a woman will not take over other men and crush their authority. She will honor and respect their leadership, while they are called to respect and honor her callings.

The blend of masculine and feminine qualities is shown very clearly throughout Scripture.

Proverbs 31:25-26 says, "She is clothed with strength and dignity, and she laughs without fear of the future. [masculine] When she speaks, her words are wise, and she gives instructions with kindness. [feminine]"

1 Timothy 3:2-3 says, "So an elder must be a man whose life is above reproach. He must be faithful to his wife. He must exercise self-control, live wisely, and have a good reputation. He must enjoy having guests in his home, and he must be able to teach. He must not be...violent. He must be gentle, not quarrelsome, and not love money."

Men and women are called to exercise both-and qualities, not either-or. Both masculine and feminine qualities.

God is revealed in the Scriptures as possessing a perfect blend of strength and softness. He is both masculine and feminine.

70

Isaiah 66:12-13 says, "This is what the Lord says: 'I will give Jerusalem a river of peace and prosperity. The wealth of the nations will flow to her. Her children will be nursed at her breasts, carried in her arms, and held on her lap. I will comfort you there in Jerusalem as a mother comforts her child."

Isaiah 40:10-11 says, "Yes, the Sovereign Lord is coming in power. He will rule with a powerful arm. See, he brings his reward with him as he comes. He will feed his flock like a shepherd. He will carry the lambs in his arms, holding them close to his heart. He will gently lead the mother sheep with their young."

Hosea 11:8-10 says, "Oh, how can I give you up, Israel? How can I let you go? How can I destroy you like Admah or demolish you like Zeboiim? My heart is torn within me, and my compassion overflows. No, I will not unleash my fierce anger. I will not completely destroy Israel, for I am God and not a mere mortal. I am the Holy One living among you, and I will not come to destroy. For someday the people will follow me. I, the Lord, will roar like a lion."

Revelation 15:3-4 says, "Great and marvelous are your works, O Lord God, the Almighty. Just and true are your ways, O King of the nations. Who will not fear you, Lord, and glorify your name? For you alone are holy. All nations will come and worship before you, for your righteous deeds have been revealed."

God is pictured as a mother, feeding and comforting her children. He is revealed as a merciful, compassionate person, longing for healing and reconciliation. At the same time, there is no doubt that he is the one in control. He has all power and all authority, and he alone deserves the worship of every mortal man and woman.

God's Design of Femininity and Masculinity

By observing God's character, you can see how both masculinity and femininity are designed to work together. A woman who is strong without being soft is hard and unfeeling. A man who is soft without being strong is weak and ambiguous. Tipping the scale in either direction causes only confusion and chaos. True femininity is not limiting. It is not unnatural. It is not victim minded.

1 Corinthians 11:3 says, "The head of every man is Christ, the head of woman is man, and the head of Christ is God."

Masculinity and femininity are about relationships. If you think that you can redefine masculinity and femininity, you will redefine God.

God is the "Alpha and the Omega - the beginning and the end" (Revelation 1:8). Whatever masculinity and femininity mean, it must start with God. God encapsulates everything. His design is illustrated by a circle.

God is the head of everything. He surrounds and embraces it all.

God's power and love encapsulates Jesus, and through him, God's power and love encapsulates all his creation, including men and women.

God surrounds Jesus= Jesus surrounds the man= the man surrounds the woman= the woman is completely protected.

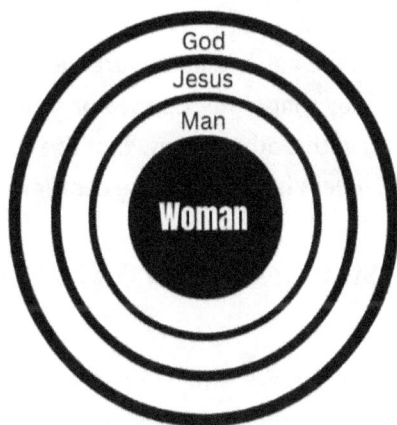

Jesus is the perfect demonstration of God's character. God's feminine and masculine sides were revealed through Jesus. He is the representation of the strength and the softness of God. Colossians 1:15-16 says, "Christ is the visible image of the invisible God. He existed before anything was created and is supreme over all creation, for through him God created everything in the heavenly realms and on earth."

In the beginning, God created people to be perfect, just like Jesus. He made the man and the woman to perfectly reflect himself, and they had a perfect relationship with him.

The beautiful thing about God's design is that it places the woman directly in the center of himself, where she is the most protected. He is her protector. He is everything she needs.

This is why, in the garden, Satan targeted her. He knew that she held the key that either opened or shut the door to close communion with God. He knew that the circle was unable to break, unless he went for the center of it.

Satan's Strategy to Ruin God's Design

Satan aroused her desires. He made her feel that God was being unfair to her, and that what God was keeping back from her wouldn't harm her but enlighten her.

Genesis 3:6 says, "The woman was convinced. She saw that the tree was beautiful and its fruit looked delicious, and she wanted the wisdom it would give her."

Sure, the fruit itself was harmless, but the desire was the poison. The desire to reach out her hand, take that delicious fruit, and enjoy its forbidden flavor. The desire to do what *she* wanted. The desire to be in control. The desire to "be like God, knowing both good and evil." (Genesis 3:5) Verse 6 says, "So she took some of the fruit and ate it. Then she gave some to her husband, who was with her, and he ate it, too."

Satan's arrow was through the heart. He had successfully poisoned God's perfect relationship with the man and the woman. From the center, the break started, and continued through the circle, cracking through the layers. When it reached Jesus, the division was complete. His perfection was untarnished, but the relationship with his creation was ruined.

The Results of the Poison

Genesis 3:7 says, "At that moment their eyes were opened, and they suddenly felt shame at their nakedness. So they sewed fig leaves together to cover themselves."

The desire that produced the action instantly introduced chaos and confusion into their perfect world. Everything changed. They didn't want to be with God anymore. Genesis 3:8-13, 16-19 says, "When the cool evening breezes were blowing, the man and his wife heard the Lord God walking about in the garden. So they hid from the Lord God among the trees. Then the Lord God called to the man, 'Where are you?' He replied, 'I heard you walking in the garden, so I hid. I was afraid because I was naked.' 'Who told you that you were naked?' the Lord God asked. 'Have you eaten from the tree whose fruit I commanded you not to eat?' The man replied, 'It was the woman you gave me who gave me the fruit, and I ate it.' Then the Lord God asked the woman, 'What have you done?' 'The serpent deceived me,' she replied. 'That's why I ate it.' ... Then he said to the woman, 'I will sharpen the pain of your pregnancy, and in pain you will give birth. And you will desire to control your husband, but he will rule over you.' And to the man he said, 'Since you listened to your wife and ate from the tree whose fruit I commanded you not to eat, the ground is cursed because of you. All your life you will struggle to scratch a living from it. It will grow thorns and thistles for you, though you will eat of its grains. By the sweat of your brow will you have food to eat until you return to the ground from which you were made. For you were made from dust, and to dust you will return.'"

The temptation that each of us faces is to blame. The poison of sin covers our eyes to see our own sin. Each of us is responsible for our own choices. The minute that we try to place the blame on either the man or the woman, we are missing the point. It's about my heart and your heart being transformed by the love of Jesus and learning to forgive, not to point fingers.

The man ate the fruit as well because he wasn't God. He was a human. And that is still the situation!

Jezebel & Ahab

Another woman in the Bible who used control and manipulation over her husband was Ahab's wife, Jezebel. Her name means "an impudent, shameless, or morally unrestrained woman." Her story is found in 1 Kings 21.

The Jezebel of the Bible story died a gruesome death. However, her legacy remains through the spirit of Jezebel. Not necessarily the spirit of Ahab's wife, but a demonic stronghold with very specific traits that match the wife of Ahab's character. It is much more sinister and dangerous than she was. It is embedding itself deeply into Western culture. It is wreaking havoc on marriages, sex, femininity, masculinity, in fact, nearly every aspect of our lives.

Jesus gave this message to the church in Revelation 2:20-23, "But I have this complaint against you. You are permitting that woman - that Jezebel who calls herself a prophet - to lead my servants astray. She teaches them to commit sexual sin and to eat food offered to idols. I gave her time to repent, but she does not want to turn away from her immorality. Therefore, I will throw her on a bed of suffering, and those who commit adultery with her will suffer greatly unless they repent and turn away from her evil deeds. I will strike her children dead. Then all the churches will know that I am the one who searches out the thoughts and intentions of every person. And I will give to each of you whatever you deserve."

- Jezebel is manipulative
- Jezebel is controlling
- Jezebel is not a worshiper of God. She may appear to be sincere, but the fruit of her heart is anything but.
- Jezebel divides relationships, especially churches and marriages.
- Jezebel is unrepentant
- Jezebel is destructive
- Jezebel feeds on the victim mindset in others, especially men.
- Jezebel creates confusion for her agenda to be carried out.
- Jezebel is unfaithful

- Jezebel causes spiritual death.

How does Jezebel come into a person's life?

Jezebel starts with seeds of fear. A woman who is afraid to trust men, who wants to be in control because she wants her own way and is afraid to lose it. Jezebel also comes in through disappointment, when a man may have hurt you, taken advantage of you, betrayed you, or didn't meet your expectations. Festering bitterness condones the victim mindset, which she lives on.

Jezebel hates femininity. She hates compassion, softness, nurturing. She takes, through manipulation, all the masculine qualities of strength and power to carry out her twisted agenda and for that, she needs a man who is weak in his masculinity.

Jezebel plays on the humanity of men.

Men are not perfect. Jezebel is extremely tricky, sneaky, and sinister, and she will use any means necessary to weaken men. It is much harder for her to control a man who has authority from his position in Christ. A man whose head is Christ will be difficult for her to deceive. However, a man who is weak-minded will be her target.

Jezebel often attacks in religion. Religion is not where Jesus is first; it is where man's rules come first, so she can easily squirm her way in somewhere, one way or another. It is an easy place for her to take control of men, because unfortunately, religious men do not have strong authority in Christ.

The Jezebel of the Bible story had a weak-minded, evil husband named Ahab. 1 Kings 16:30-31 says, "But Ahab son of Omri did what was evil in the Lord's sight, even more than any of the kings before him. And as though it were not enough to follow the example of Jeroboam, he married Jezebel, the daughter of King Ethbaal of the Sidonians, and he began to bow down in worship of Baal."

Unfortunately, the spirit of Ahab still exists as well. Today, it is the spirit of Jezebel which attacks and undermines men's authority, and it is the spirit of Ahab which enables and encourages the Jezebel spirit. Ahab is fuel for Jezebel. He is the embers which she can stoke and use to burn him to death.

The redefinition of femininity and masculinity is nothing more than a removal of God.

But there is a better way. The truth is that God cannot be removed. He cannot be changed. He cannot be redefined. He will bring judgment on those who choose to disobey and do not repent.

Those who choose to obey God will discover his blessing on them as they work together and not against each other. Proverbs 31:11-12 says, "Her husband can trust her, and she will greatly enrich his life. She brings him good, not harm, all the days of her life."

1 Corinthians 11:12 says, "For although the first woman came from man, every other man was born from a woman, and everything comes from God."

In other words, men and women are equal in value before God. It is the victim mindset that says that women are less than men. 1 Peter 3:7 says that "She may be weaker than you are, but she is your equal partner in God's gift of new life." "Weaker" does not mean "less than." "Weaker" means that she is fully embracing her feminine quality of dependence. She is not self-sufficient. The woman, in the context of marriage, cannot bring life into the world by herself. She needs her husband to help her create life. It is also true that she needs her husband to support her in every area. This weakness is a strength when she allows herself to receive, because that is who she is as a woman. This is what allows her and her husband to receive God's gift of new life. Those who reject this message do not receive life.

Men and women are not alike. We have different responsibilities, callings, and personalities. We look, act, and think differently. We are each made differently on purpose, by design, by an intelligent Creator. He made us in his image. But the moment we allow those differences to make us feel as though the one is superior, that is when we have stepped out of the place where God has put us. God gave us those differences; when we accept them, we can see each other as equally needed for the work that God has given each of us to do.

As I have been writing this chapter, Satan has been attacking me, specifically in my view of men. He knows that this is an area in my life where I have been wounded, and he attacks using all the lies and fears I used to live with. I began to behave toward my husband in a controlling, manipulative way. I didn't realize what was happening until I stopped and looked at the connection between what I am writing and the nature of the attacks. Again, this is a subject that Satan does not want me to write about, but that only gives me more reason to do it! Women need to know that it is possible to relate to men in a godly way.

Godly Femininity in Action

Philippians 2:1-11 says, "Is there any encouragement from belonging to Christ? Any comfort from his love? Any fellowship together in the Spirit? Are your hearts tender and compassionate? Then make me truly happy by agreeing wholeheartedly with each other, loving one another, and working together with one mind and purpose. Don't be selfish; don't try to impress others. Be humble, thinking of others as better than yourselves. Don't look out only for your own interests, but take an interest in others, too. You must have the same attitude that Christ Jesus had. Though he was God, he did not think of equality with God as something to cling to. Instead, he gave up his divine privileges; he took the humble position of a slave and was born as a human being. When he appeared in human form, he humbled himself in obedience to God and died a criminal's death on a cross. Therefore, God elevated him to the place of highest honor and gave him the name above all other names, that at the name of Jesus every knee should bow, in heaven and on earth and under the earth, and every tongue confess that Jesus Christ is Lord, to the glory of God the Father."

Jesus gave us a pattern of servant hood to follow.

There are many men who are not safe to trust, and we need to be aware and discern who the good ones are. We should not blindly trust men. But when a woman cannot trust a godly man, there is a problem.

The way to process trust issues with men is our map:
Reveal the lies.

Release the lies.

Replace with truth.

Restore.

Honesty is like putting your wounds under a magnifying glass. It's incredibly humbling. But the hope is found in that Jesus bore those wounds to the cross. We don't need to relate to men from a wounded standpoint. In Jesus, my heart is healed. I can relate to men from a healed heart. I can see them with healed vision. No longer do I need to protect myself from men. I am protected, because I am protected in Christ.

The problem is not that men have hurt you. The problem is that lies are allowed to cloud your vision and twist your view of men.

There are three things that women can do which will greatly improve relationships with men and restore them to the place where God designed them to be - not under men, but inside of their protection.

#1 Forgive

Matthew 6:14-15 says, "If you forgive those who sin against you, your heavenly Father will forgive you. But if you refuse to forgive others, your Father will not forgive your sins."

God's character requires that we live in alignment with his commandments. Light and darkness cannot coexist. Forgiveness is not unfair. When Jesus hung on the cross, bleeding, suffocating, naked, he said, "Father, forgive them, for they don't know what they are doing." (Luke 23:34)

Nothing will test the quality of your character more than the act of forgiveness. Hebrews 12:15 says, "Watch out that no poisonous root of bitterness grows up to trouble you, corrupting many." A root is hidden, beneath the surface, in your heart. It may be kept secret for a while, but a root must have a stem above the surface. The root doesn't stay with you; as it grows, it spreads and contaminates others around you. Bitterness is truly toxic.

Forgiveness is the best method to overcome the victim mindset. It has been one of the most powerful, life-transforming choices I have ever made, because every time I choose to forgive, it brings me closer and closer to God.

Bitterness fuels Jezebel. Bitterness fuels feminism. It is time to rise up and stop the poison of death spreading over our world, with forgiveness.

#2 Serve

Serving is the secret to beautiful relationships. It is a by-product of forgiveness. It is the practical expression of love. It is the choice to be understanding, kind, and patient, regardless of your feelings or others' actions.

John 15:13 says, "There is no greater love than to lay down one's life for one's friends." Serving does *not* make you a doormat. Serving means that you take your qualities, your feminine strengths and your masculine undertones and you use them to bless others. Both men and women are given a space to occupy, a voice to use, talents, dreams. Be willing to bless the gift and voice in the men around you. Be willing to be the spark that gets their fires burning. This is love: laying down your life for your friends. If it puts you into the background, remember that you're a servant, not a victim. Victims become angry that they're not in the spotlight and begin to fight and control. You are not obliterated by serving. A godly man will feel honored by being served and will return the honor. Men aren't perfect, but they need to know that women respect and honor them. When a woman steps into the background and serves, it fuels her voice, her calling, her passion.

#3 Pray

Prayer is a great way to serve. Prayer is not a way to get what we want. Servants are willing to do the dirty work of fighting in prayer, not fighting to be seen. When women are faithful to pray, those women will be seen and celebrated by Jesus. What you do behind the scenes will have consequences, whether it is a hidden root of bitterness or a choice to lay down yourself for others.

If what God wants for men is different from what I want, then I need to examine my motives and realign my perspective. If men were as women wanted, they would be petty, weak, and soft. Men need women to let them be strong protectors, but women also need to let men mess up, learn, and try again. If I want men to give me grace as a woman, I need to offer them that same privilege. If I see something in a man that needs to be changed, I will have the greatest effect on him by talking to God about it. No one can effectively produce change in a man, except for God. If your heart is in alignment with God's heart, and you are praying prayers in line with the Spirit, he will listen and he has the power to work miracles in hearts that seem impossibly hard.

A quick note to married women:

Submission starts in your mind. If Satan can get you to think and believe a lie, he will be able to cause division. One of the best things you can do for your husband is to examine your behavior and trace it back to your mind to discover if any lies you are believing are manifesting in controlling behavior. Submission is another method of serving. The church submits to Christ because he died for them. The church knows what they've been given: Jesus. In your marriage, your husband gives himself to you, and you receive him and his love. You also give yourself to him, and he also receives you. It is a cycle of masculine and feminine qualities working together.

You are not devalued by submission. If your husband feels the need to fight you for him to do his calling, you are out of place as his wife. You are equal in value, but your differences demand that you need to step back and give him space. When you do this, it frees him up to lead and to love you. Because he loves you, he will give you the freedom to do your part. It is like a dance, and when you step in harmony, it works. Fighting between ourselves is a trick of the enemy to weaken unity. It distracts us from fighting him.

Men and women are the best physical representations of God's character in His creation. The reason there is so much confusion and fighting is that we fail to recognize God in each other. Let's learn to love, because God is love.

Exercises

#1 Reveal

What am I feeling right now?

Why am I feeling this way?

What lies am I believing?

Where do the lies come from?

What am I allowing to control my mind?

What shuts me down?

What causes me to stop dreaming?

What is my biggest fear?

#2 Release

This step is all about creating awareness. When you have lived for a long time with habits of thinking a certain way, it requires a commitment to daily train yourself to think differently-not an easy task. Catch yourself in the act of believing a lie. Don't let the lie go. It's easy to slip, especially in the beginning. The beginning is the hardest.

Find the Scripture verses that speak to the lies in your head. I have often turned on audio Scriptures when Satan was fighting to shut my mouth. Not today, Satan!

Speak those verses out loud. The louder, the better. I remember many car drives when I would use the time to really get the words out with volume. Spoken words shift the atmosphere drastically. Satan hears what you say. Say it as though you believe it! Take authority over your mind.

Journal section:

Bible verses:

#3 Replace

Once you have become honest about your struggles, and you are working to create awareness where you need to change your belief systems, you need to replace the lies with the truth.

This is a constant process. Your brain has literal grooves in it from thinking the same way for so long. It takes time and repetition to change it, to create new grooves. This is where the bigger tests happen.

Replacing the lies with the truth happens when you constantly, with awareness and intention, tell yourself something different. It won't happen by accident. It won't happen by itself. It takes work. Especially when you are struggling with a lie, that is when you need to tell yourself the truth.

Journal section:

#4 Forgive

Forgiveness is often pure choice. It rarely has anything to do with feelings. In fact, you may still feel anger and hatred. But in the middle of feeling angry and hateful, the choice to forgive has the power to break those chains. Only Jesus has the power to help you to choose forgiveness through heated emotions.

Journal section:

Who do I need to forgive?

For what do I need to forgive?

CHAPTER 5

WHAT YOUR BODY MEANS: HOW TO GLORIFY GOD WITH YOUR BODY

"My dove is hiding behind the rocks, behind an outcrop on the cliff. Let me see your face; let me hear your voice. For your voice is pleasant, and your face is lovely." Song of Solomon 2:14

The first time that my husband (then boyfriend) Mike told me that I was cute was on our first date. We were sitting next to the river in Old Sacramento, which became one of our favorite and most memorable date areas. The Tower Bridge reflected sparkling gold on the flowing water. The rustic boardwalks provided ample space to go for walks, and our favorite coffee shop, Steamers, was situated conveniently on a corner where we could sit and talk on Sunday mornings.

But that first time was extremely nerve-wracking. I was very insecure and lacked self-confidence. I still believed a lot of lies about myself and I was afraid of men. Even though I trusted Mike and I knew that he was safe, I couldn't let down my guard, yet. When he dared to tell me that he found me attractive, I shut down. It was, in my mind, as though he'd declared me ugly, because that was the lie underneath my wall.

As our relationship progressed, I had to do a lot of homework. I learned very quickly that lies that I believed about myself did a lot of harm and damage to our relationship. In fact, dating and marriage forced me to process lies that I didn't even know I believed about myself. It has continued in this way ever since our wedding day. It is a continuous process of becoming vulnerable by opening myself up to the truth about myself.

The Lie That Says "I Am Not Beautiful"

I came from a culture of religion with a huge emphasis on the negativity and pridefulness of beauty. I was taught that it was humbler and godlier to be ugly than to be attractive. I always felt deep shame about being a woman and having a woman's body. Wearing long dresses and covering my hair was the definition of modesty. But if God created me to be a woman, why did I have to hide my womanhood? Why did I want to be beautiful if being beautiful was proud? I labeled my feminine desires as "selfish" and "proud," but then I felt completely worthless as a woman.

I felt like my womanly body was in the way. If I could remove my feminine characteristics, wouldn't that take care of the problem? I didn't want to change my gender. But I thought that there must be something intrinsically wrong with me, because I wanted to be beautiful! No matter how much I told myself that that desire was wrong, it never went away. I always told myself that nobody would want to marry me, because I had nothing to attract anyone. And if attraction was bad, I would do everything I could to avoid it. But then I was afraid I had sinned if I wanted to get married.

It was a vicious cycle. I knew I had to leave religion in order to break it. So, I did. And the cycle was broken.

Making God Look Good

Once I began to be mentored and trained in the ways of God, I discovered many things that surprised me. For the first time ever, I was allowed to explore and to ask questions. I could be honest about how I felt.

I realized that by trying to erase my feminine desire to be beautiful, I had shut down and blocked off my dreams, my passion, my purpose. I had tried to re-make my femininity and how I am hard-wired as a woman. If God created me to be beautiful, then the ugliness was nothing but lies, shame, insecurity, and self-hatred.

But then I discovered something else. The desire to be beautiful, the dream to get married, and even my body wasn't meant to be about myself. I wasn't meant to be beautiful for me. I wasn't meant to get married for me. My body wasn't for me. Why did I want these things in the first place? It all started with a God who had a dream of a bride. He had a picture in his mind of her radiance and loveliness - but it wasn't her own beauty. It was a reflection of his glory.

You and I are that bride.

If I am engaged to God, then to use what he has given me for my own pleasure is adultery. God created beauty, marriage, and femininity as tools to bring him glory. God created me to know himself just like a man desires to know his wife. God created me to care about his glory and to make him look good. This is the purpose of the dreams and desires. It's not about me. It's about him.

1 Corinthians 10:31 says, "Whatever you do, do it all for the glory of God."

1 Corinthians 6:19-20 says, "Don't you realize that your body is the temple of the Holy Spirit, who lives in you and was given to you by God? You do not belong to yourself, for God bought you with a high price. So you must honor God with your body."

I began to understand that God has a plan for my body. I began to allow God to strip away the shame and the negative mindsets that I had created about my body. I began to see God in a new light. I began to recognize him as the Creator of my body and that my body was meant to physically represent himself.

My body was no longer in the way. It was becoming a tool for the glory of God.

In order to understand the truth about myself, I had to evaluate my internal voice. What did I tell myself about myself? What did I believe about myself? This internal voice had been shaped by what I'd heard my whole life from my outer environment. As I examined it, I had to deal with huge loads of self-hatred. I thought I couldn't stand myself.

We have already talked about the process of overcoming self-hatred, but I will just say this. If I am designed to make God look good, then to hate myself meant that I wasn't in agreement with what he says about me. I wasn't glorifying him. I wasn't making him look good. I was calling what he created and called good a lie.

Self-hatred is completely against who I am as a woman. It hinders femininity because it makes you act roughly and insensitively. Why? Because you feel all tense inside. Your heart feels bunched up, choked by fear.

So, I followed the map:

Reveal the lies.

Release the lies.

Replace with truth.

Restore with forgiveness.

Forgiveness was one of the biggest tools for me in this process. I had literally been taught to view myself negatively. A lot of my shame and insecurity came from my outer environment. I internalized the voices around me, and they became my belief systems and thought patterns. When God began to show me what he thought about me, I couldn't believe it at first because it was so drastically different from what I thought about myself. My breakthrough happened when I forgave the people who were responsible for my outer environment. This enabled me to take responsibility for my negative beliefs and to change my situation.

Forgiveness is the door leading to a healthy view of yourself. Forgiveness takes you from a victim mindset to a victorious one. Forgiveness enables you to make empowered decisions, to walk in freedom, to take responsibility for yourself. It is the ultimate way to make God look good. It is the doorway to true beauty.

The Beauty of God's Character

I began to learn how God sees beauty. He saw me as beautiful long before I did. He saw me at a heart level. He saw me for who I was. He loved me for who I was. Even though I am not perfect, he sees that I have a heart that genuinely wants to please him. He meets my sin with grace - not judgment. That is the most beautiful thing in the world.

God is perfectly beautiful. There is no way that I can be as beautiful as he is. But the wonderful thing is that his grace changed my heart. He took me, in my ugly sin, and transformed me. I couldn't stay in my selfishness and be alive in him. For those who refuse to obey, there is judgment. But those who really love him will choose to be humbled and changed by his grace.

This is God's character - to take mere people who have sinned against him and show them mercy and grace and love. He gives us an opportunity to know him. Every day, his mercy is new. Every day, his patience is fresh. Let us not test his patience by staying fixed on worldly things. Let us fix our eyes on him.

Colossians 3:1-4 says, "Since you have been raised to new life with Christ, set your sights on the realities of heaven, where Christ sits in the place of honor at God's right hand. Think about the things of heaven, not the things of earth. For you died to this life, and your real life is hidden with Christ in God. And when Christ, who is your life, is revealed to the whole world, you will share in all his glory."

God began to teach me that this is how he wants me to live - with grace. He wants the way that I think and behave to reflect his character, not the way that the world thinks and behaves. His character is expressed in how he made me. My femininity is created to resemble God's heart. He put a piece of himself into every single person. He made me who I am because of who he is.

Psalm 139:1 says, "O Lord, you have examined my heart and know everything about me."

This verse is beautiful because it displays the heart posture God wants you to have. Complete openness, complete vulnerability, complete honesty. God sees you and me from the inside out. He doesn't compare my hair color with yours. He sees my tendency to compare myself to others. He sees my sin of jealousy of someone else. This is the amazing thing: he doesn't condemn me. He calls me into his arms, and whispers, "Rest, daughter. Let me fill your emptiness. I am enough."

When people failed me, I had to learn to not reflect those broken expectations back to God. He calls himself Father, Husband, Lover. If I wanted to know God in this way, I had to release the failures of people and expect the goodness of God to come through the brokenness. My view of myself and my perception of God is intricately connected to and deeply affected by other people's behavior. This is why forgiveness and releasing people is so important.

When you can see that God is always good no matter what people around you do, you are free. You can be confident because your joy and security isn't based on people or their actions; it is found in God. That place of rest, security, and confidence is where true beauty comes from. You can be completely honest with God because he already knows your heart anyway!

Psalm 139:17 says, "How precious are your thoughts about me, O God. They cannot be numbered! I can't even count them; they outnumber the grains of sand! And when I wake up, you are still with me!"

Did you know that God is obsessed with you? He is crazy about you. His thoughts about you can't even be counted. He thinks about you constantly. Imagine trying to count grains of sand. That is what it's like trying to count God's thoughts about you. It's not just a dream either! It's not too good to be true!

You are not forgotten.

You are not alone.

You are not forsaken.

You are created to live in this place of openness with God. He is where your life and your beauty are meant to flow from. He is where your eyes are opened to see how his character is expressed in your physical body.

The Choice to Glorify God

In all of creation, God made everything as a mirror so that we would look at it and see who he is. He wants us to be constantly reminded of him. He wants us to look at the sky and see his limitless love. He wants us to think of him when we see a flower, a playful squirrel, a newborn baby, a glorious sunset. God thinks of us constantly; he wants to remind us to think of him constantly.

Romans 1:19-20 says, "They know the truth about God because he has made it obvious to them. For ever since the world was created, people have seen the earth and sky. Through everything God made, they can clearly see his invisible qualities - his eternal power and divine nature. So they have no excuse for not knowing God."

Psalm 19:1-4 says, "The heavens proclaim the glory of God. The skies display his craftsmanship. Day after day they continue to speak; night after night they make him known. They speak without a sound or word; their voice is never heard. Yet their message has gone throughout the earth, and their words to all the world."

God is right in front of us. He is not the one who is lost. He is not the one who needs to change. He must get glory. Those who do not choose to glorify him will receive judgment.

Luke 19:29-40 says, "As he came to the towns of Bethphage and Bethany on the Mount of Olives, he sent two disciples ahead. 'Go into that village over there,' he told them. 'As you enter it, you will see a young donkey tied there that no one has ever ridden. Untie it and bring it here. If anyone asks, "Why are you untying that colt?" just say, "The Lord needs it."' So they went and found the colt, just as Jesus had said. And sure enough, as they were untying it, the owners asked them, 'Why are you untying that colt?' And the disciples simply replied, 'The Lord needs it.' So they brought the colt to Jesus and threw their garments over it for him to ride on. As he rode along, the crowds spread out their garments on the road ahead of him. When he reached the place where the road started down the Mount of Olives, all of his followers began to shout and sing as they walked along, praising God for all the wonderful miracles they had seen.

'Blessings on the King who comes in the
name of the Lord!
Peace in heaven, and glory in highest
heaven!'
But some of the Pharisees among the crowd said, 'Teacher, rebuke your followers for saying things like that!'

He replied, 'If they kept quiet, the stones along the road would burst into cheers!'"

The difference between people and the rest of creation is that creation does not have a choice but to glorify God. This is why the sun rises and sets every day, the flowers bloom and die, the wind blows and falls. If creation could rebel, there would not be the order, grandeur, wonder, beauty and awe to experience.

We, as people with souls and created in God's image, have a choice to make. Creation has a purpose, including us. God created us with a calling on our lives: to glorify him. He gives us the choice whether or not we will carry it out. But my life has a calling on it to serve him, and he has given me everything I need to do it.

He has given me my body to serve his purposes in my life. My body is created to reflect his glory. My body is designed to be God's instrument and his tool. He wants me to look at myself and see him. He wants me to know him through my body, because my body is his creation. My body is created to physically represent God.

In Jesus' time, the Pharisees were the religious leaders who said with their words that they obeyed God but had no evidence of obedience in how they lived. Jesus called them more hard-hearted than the stones along the road. The Pharisees saw Jesus and did not believe that he was the Messiah. They didn't want to see him, because he called them out on their lifestyles. They didn't want to believe a man who would call them to change.

Jesus says in Matthew 23:25-26, "What sorrow awaits you teachers of religious law and you Pharisees. Hypocrites! For you are so careful to clean the outside of the cup and the dish, but inside you are filthy - full of greed and self-indulgence! You blind Pharisee! First wash the inside of the cup and the dish, and then the outside will become clean, too."

The religious law does nothing to clean your heart. The only thing that can cleanse a sinful heart is the blood of Jesus. The only thing that can give you power over sin is the Holy Spirit.

In order to have a sacred flow of beauty coming from that inner place in your heart, your inner heart must be cleansed. True beauty is vulnerable. True beauty is honest. True beauty is holy. True beauty is a lifestyle that comes from a heart soft and pliable to the loveliness of Jesus. True beauty can be developed, grown, produced. It is the fruit of a heart close to Jesus.

God's heart is beautiful, and when you come to him with an open heart, honest and broken by your sin, he redeems you and places a crown of royalty on your head. He clothes you with himself. Just as a bride on her wedding day shows her purity by wearing white, so God has created your outward body to be a representation of your inward heart. You are God's bride. You embody God's heart. You are a picture of heaven on earth.

Isaiah 61:3, 10 says, "To all who mourn in Israel, he will give a crown of beauty for ashes, a joyous blessing instead of mourning, festive praise instead of despair... I am overwhelmed with joy in the Lord my God! For he has dressed me with the clothing of salvation and draped me in a robe of righteousness. I am like a bridegroom in his wedding suit or a bride with her jewels."

Isaiah 62:2-4 says, "You will be given a new name by the Lord's own mouth. The Lord will hold you in his hand for all to see - a splendid crown in the hand of God. Never again will you be called 'The Forsaken City' or 'The Desolate Land.' Your new name will be 'The City of God's Delight' and 'The Bride of God,' for the Lord delights in you and will claim you as his bride."

Intimacy with God is the way to make the connection between inward and outward beauty. Any blocks, lies, or lack of vulnerability will hinder the intimacy, which will hold back the inward beauty from flowing out. In order to be intimate with God, the lies must be removed and replaced with truth. It is again the map leading to the treasure inside:

Reveal the lies (honesty)
Release the lies (bind the lies)
Replace with truth
Restore (forgive)
Now you are free to see yourself as he sees you.

I spent years wrestling in agony about who I was and where I belonged. As my heart opened up towards God, I slowly learned how to rest my fears. Marriage taught me many lessons about this. Insecurity is the enemy of intimacy. I had to learn to believe that I am as beautiful as my husband says I am. Anything else is a lie. In marriage, my body represents my calling. I am called to receive love and produce the fruit of it. It is the same way with God. He created me to receive his love and produce the fruit of it. Marriage intimacy is an extension of the way that God loves us.

It doesn't require being married to know God's love for you in this way. This is how he loves every one of us. God created women physically as an expression of part of his heart. His feminine nature is expressed tangibly in us. A woman is designed to be elegant, graceful, and feminine because this is how she best reflects God's image. Femininity is not a prison; it is a way of living full of joy, rest, and love because you are not your own. You are his. You are his treasure, pride, and joy.

How to Accept Your Body to Glorify God

Psalm 139:13-14 says, "You made all the delicate, inner parts of my body and knit me together in my mother's womb. Thank you for making me so wonderfully complex! Your workmanship is marvelous - how well I know it."

He created every part of your body for a purpose.

Your features, the shape of your nose, your jawline is made specifically for you. The very details of freckles or hair color shows God's attention to the small things about you. If you are like most women, there is something about yourself that you don't like. But the Lover of your soul and the Creator of your body is the same being, and he invites you to go to him with your struggle to accept your physical traits. This is a huge part of being honest with God and experiencing intimacy with him. He already knows how you feel. It's up to you to get honest about it.

When Jesus came to earth, he went into the temple and cleansed it of the people buying and selling animals for sacrifice. Matthew 21:13 says, "He said to them, 'The Scriptures declare, "My temple will be called a house of prayer," but you have turned it into a den of thieves!'"

The temple had been turned into a place of greed and jealousy. The sacrifices of the animals were no longer pure. These people were stealing the glory of God with the money they earned. All they wanted was to get rich.

Now that Jesus has died for us, our bodies are his temple. The Holy Spirit lives inside of us. So many times, we are guilty of taking his sacrifice and selling it for our own glory. We don't believe what God says about us, because we don't like what he does.

I had to get honest with how I felt about my physical body. There were many things I didn't like. I asked myself:

Do I really trust God?

Do I really believe him?

Believing negative things about your body produces negative emotions about yourself, which causes you to behave in negative ways. Lies actually make you look less attractive! A lot of my negative mindsets about myself went even deeper, to my negative mindset towards God. I had to admit that I didn't believe or trust him. So much breakthrough for me happened when I forgave God. Forgiving him was crucial. It completely changed my view of him and took away the barriers I held against him. Suddenly, I was set free to see myself with no shame - the way he sees me.

When you struggle to accept any part of your body, bring it to Jesus. Release him of your perceived idea of who he is and let him show himself to you. Don't let people destroy your connection with God. He is bigger than what anyone may have done or said to you.

This is where your body finds freedom. Tension is released. New life is born. Beauty glows on your face, from that inner place. Claim every single part of your body for Jesus. Throw the lies into the trash and replace them with the words of God. Purposely, intentionally speak truth over your body. Take back what was stolen by Satan and use it for God.

This is where you will discover how your physical body represents your calling. As you do the things which contribute to the attributes you want, you'll find out who you are.

What Your Physical Body Represents

One of the most intimate books of the Bible is the Song of Solomon. This is where God reveals himself as a passionate bridegroom, in pursuit of his lovely bride. This is what we are created for, single or married - to be in love with our Lover.

Song of Solomon 4:1-5 says, "You are beautiful, my darling, beautiful beyond words. Your eyes are like doves behind your veil. Your hair falls in waves, like a flock of goats winding down the slopes of Gilead. Your teeth are as white as sheep, recently shorn and freshly washed. Your smile is flawless, each tooth matched with its twin. Your lips are like scarlet ribbon; your mouth is inviting. Your cheeks are like rosy pomegranates behind your veil. Your neck is as beautiful as the tower of David, jeweled with the shields of a thousand heroes. Your breasts are like two fawns, twin fawns of a gazelle grazing among the lilies."

The author is not merely comparing his bride with animals. He is describing her character.

Eyes	⟶	Doves
Hair	⟶	Goats
Teeth	⟶	Sheep, white, clean
Smile	⟶	Flawless
Lips	⟶	Red ribbon, inviting
Cheeks	⟶	Rosy pomegranates
Neck	⟶	Tower of David
Breasts	⟶	Two fawns of a gazelle

Doves (her eyes) are a symbol of the Holy Spirit.

Goat (her hair) means "strength." Goats were important in this culture for their milk and meat for food and their hair for clothes.

Sheep (her teeth) are followers. They need a shepherd. (see John 10) White and clean symbolizes purity. Sheep were also valuable for their wool, meat, and milk.

Red ribbon (her lips) symbolizes passion.

Pomegranates (her cheeks) traditionally symbolize fertility and love.

The tower of David (her neck) was a place of protection for the city, a place of defense.

Twin fawns of a gazelle (her breasts) refer to motherhood and marriage. A child finds his mother's breasts comforting. They symbolize blessing, satisfaction, love, gentleness, grace.

Song of Solomon 4:1-5 paraphrased:

"You are beautiful, my darling, beautiful beyond words. You have spiritual wisdom and discernment. It is the source of all your character. You are a strong woman, and you provide well for those in your care. You love Jesus and know that you need him. He is the one who provides what you need. He is the one who purifies you and sustains you. You are perfect, as your God is. You are alive. You are full of life. You do not allow pain to take away your dreams. You keep going even when it hurts. You love deeply and fully. You are loved deeply and fully. You are a warrior, a place of safety for those in your responsibility. You fight for what matters. You are a blessing, and you bring blessing to every single person, every day. I am satisfied to spend the rest of my life with you."

The Eyes of the Holy Spirit

John 14:16-17 says, "And I will ask the Father, and he will give you another Advocate, who will never leave you. He is the Holy Spirit, who leads into all truth. The world cannot receive him, because it isn't looking for him and doesn't recognize him. But you know him, because he lives with you now and later will be in you."

John 3:3-8 says, "Jesus replied, 'I tell you the truth, unless you are born again, you cannot see the Kingdom of God.' 'What do you mean?' exclaimed Nicodemus. 'How can an old man go back into his mother's womb and be born again?' Jesus replied, 'I assure you, no one can enter the Kingdom of God without being born of water and the Spirit. Humans can reproduce only human life, but the Holy Spirit gives birth to spiritual life. So don't be surprised when I say, "You must be born again." The wind blows wherever it wants. Just as you can hear the wind but can't tell where it comes from or where it is going, so you can't explain how people are born of the Spirit.'"

Those who look at life with only their physical eyes see only physical things. They are limited to what is around them, to what they perceive to be true, to be only human. But they are blind to the truth. Only the Holy Spirit can take away their blindness and liberate them from themselves. He alone can give the eyes to see into the spiritual realm, to understand what God is doing and who he wants you to be.

This is called being "born again." Jesus ascribed the feminine action of giving birth to the Holy Spirit. Unless you allow yourself to be re-born, to let go of yourself and let the Spirit do his work, you can't see yourself properly. Only he has the eyes to see and the wisdom to teach you who he is and who you are. Trying to control the Spirit is like trying to control the wind - it's impossible.

He is the eyes through which you need to see yourself. He provides a lens of comfort, encouragement, and hope. In the middle of a fallen world, he provides the only true comfort. He is the only source of wisdom and truth. The Comforter enables you to rest, to be at peace, and this enables you to see yourself with clear vision.

The eyes of a person are either the opening or the closing to the rest of the body. The spiritual vision of a person either enables or hinders life. What do you see when you look in the mirror? What do you see when you look at your body? Is your body a place where Jesus is free to bring forth fruit?

When the Holy Spirit is giving you his vision, you will use your body to bear fruit for him. He will give birth to his beauty -

- to strength instead of weakness,
- to humility and submission instead of pride,
- to passion instead of apathy or death,
- to fruitfulness, abundance and love instead of barrenness, dryness, or coldness,

- to protection and defense rather than a victim mindset,
- to comfort, blessing, and satisfaction instead of hopelessness and despair.

A groom who is pursuing his bride wants her heart. He wants her heart to be alive to him and showing evidence of her desire for him and her faithfulness to him. This is true beauty in action. It means surrender. It means giving yourself up. It's not about you.

The Practical Outworking of Beauty

As a woman of God, what are your hands made for?

Before we were married, my husband sent this to me:

So I was thinking about how you have such beautiful hands and arms and all the sudden I remembered how in dreams and visions those things have very specific meanings and symbolism. So arms usually represent strength and hands usually represent ministering and a lot of times specifically in healing. I immediately thought of the times that you ministered strength and encouragement so well and thoroughly to me, and I totally could relate to what I felt in my spirit. It's very possible that God made it as a statement to show your assignments and what you're made to do, and who you are. Just thought I'd share that with you.

A pianist knows where to put her hands on the piano to make beautiful harmony.

An artist knows how to use her hands to create beautiful things.

A woman of God knows how to use her hands for gentleness and for showing love - the very heart of God.

Practice softness in touch. Rough touches do not communicate love.

Practice gentleness or strength in your voice, depending on which is needed.

Train your eyes and your smile to work together with your hands to portray gentleness.

The root of rough behavior is lies. Ask the Lord to show you where your heart is in your behavior. Ask the Lord to show you who you are.

"Do you believe that your feminine beauty and sexuality could bridge heaven to earth instead of earth to hell?

Your sexuality is God's gift to you. His nature is expressed through it. The pleasure, delight and intimate love He bestows on you is mirrored back to Him through your beauty and sexuality. You were created to love and be loved deeply. The ache of your heart to enjoy and be enjoyed, to know and be known is the distinct call of your Heavenly Bridegroom. Let it lead you all the way home...to Him. He made you in His image, to be a bride for Him to love. The sweet mystery of intimacy was first birthed in His own heart and then He breathed it into you that you might be drawn into this song of divine love. Relationship. Joy. Pleasure. Connection. Satisfaction. Devotion. He is the Source of all these things and because of that, He is most willing and able to restore what has been broken.

Sexual brokenness is the result of abuse or actions/relationships we were involved in for which we feel shame. Sexual brokenness can also express itself through the unhealthy teachings and ideas that have been handed to you from the generations before you or from the spiritual authorities in your life. Sexual brokenness, as with all brokenness when it is not placed on the cross and raised to new life, is imparted to those who come after us and to those around us.

Pursuing wholeness means to swim upstream against the tide of brokenness. This is no small feat, but it is a feat that is absolutely worth it. Hope is in the fact that when Jesus died and rose back to life, the miracle of redemption and wholeness was completed. Your journey to sexual wholeness is in receiving the integration of this miracle into your sexuality, until it permeates the deepest part of your soul. YOUR CONFIDENCE IN WHO JESUS MADE YOU TO BE WILL BECOME MORE FAMILIAR TO YOU THAN THE SICKNESS OF SOUL YOU PREVIOUSLY IDENTIFIED WITH. When you begin to step into alignment with the goodness and beauty that created your sexuality, you are stepping away from the lies that sabotaged it.

When you embrace your feminine beauty and sexuality with love, power and a sound mind, it's no longer the frightful, self-conscious shame and awkwardness going ahead of you into every exchange between you and men. Love is what goes before you into a room, love wraps Himself around you and it is Love that is behind you and within you. So completely perfectly loved...dare to believe it. Where shame, addiction, dissociation and self-conscious awkwardness held you hostage, Love comes and unlocks the cages, setting you free to live, serve and love wholeheartedly.

God has created you with the capacity to live wholeheartedly as a cherished daughter, a passionate lover with your husband, a nurturing mother to your children, a safe strong friend and sister, a creative woman from whose heart and hands flows a unique art that beautifies the world around you. Art is not just a paintbrush and easel. Art is the food you make, the table you spread, the house you turn into a home, the encouragement you speak, the blessing you write, the joy you splash on those in your realm, the nourishment, wisdom and strength that pours from your heart into all the big and little places that need your gift of womanhood.

It is yours, sister. Your feminine beauty and sexuality are God's gift to you, to be received with joy and stewarded with honor and delight. Experiences, mindsets and spiritual strongholds might have convinced you to dissociate yourself from parts of your body and femininity, unconsciously willing it to go away or stay dead. The brutal part of this is that you are physically alive, but carry within, deep layers of dying matter. It's a kind of brutal anguish to embody the stifled parts of us that were meant to be gloriously alive.

Would you dare to believe that He made you for good, something very, very good? And that you get to put that good garment on and wear it confidently in joyful honor to Him Who gave it to you?

There is often a great deal of fear surrounding our beliefs about our sexuality. Fear was probably imparted to you to some extent and firmly intertwined with your beliefs about your sexuality and beauty. Along with the other idols we've set up higher than God, fear is an idol we will need to repent of partnering with. We most likely also have fears about what if we get it wrong and swing wide over to the other side of the coin, where dishonor, promiscuity and disrespect destroy the value, worth and dignity God authored. Aligning our thoughts of ourselves with His thoughts of us will lead us to a deeper honor and respect for Him, ourselves and those around us. When you speak the language of honor, you are in stark contrast to the language of dishonor spoken rampantly in the world and religious groups.

The kind of reclaiming in which you know to be the work of God, falls beautifully in line with His nature. He is faithful and so we will be when we are in Him. He is pure and so will we be.

The world is dark and the forces at work in the world are dark. But let our eyes, our minds, our hearts and our souls be ever looking toward the Light, learning from it, receiving it, loving it, and becoming like it. We need to take good honest looks at the landscapes of our hearts, but we'll never possess our Canaan by continuously looking at the deprivation of our Egypt. Jesus is intimately acquainted with your pain and broken places, and He will be faithful in holding you close and leading you to new landscapes of healing and redemption. He is the choice you will never regret making. He is the One Who will give beauty for ashes and a life of wholehearted loving for one of fearful servitude.

He continues to love me into wholeness. I'm so grateful for the miracle of redemption He wrapped my battered soul in and the identity of an Overcomer He has placed on my head."

-Gloria Volkov

Exercises

#1 Reveal

What am I feeling right now?

Why am I feeling this way?

What lies am I believing?

Where do the lies come from?

What am I allowing to control my mind?

What shuts me down?

What causes me to stop dreaming?

What is my biggest fear?

#2 Release

This step is all about creating awareness. When you have lived for a long time with habits of thinking a certain way, it requires a commitment to daily train yourself to think differently-not an easy task. Catch yourself in the act of believing a lie. Don't let the lie go. It's easy to slip, especially in the beginning. The beginning is the hardest.

Find the Scripture verses that speak to the lies in your head. I have often turned on audio Scriptures when Satan was fighting to shut my mouth. Not today, Satan!

Speak those verses out loud. The louder, the better. I remember many car drives when I would use the time to really get the words out with volume. Spoken words shift the atmosphere drastically. Satan hears what you say. Say it as though you believe it! Take authority over your mind.

Journal section:

Bible verses:

#3 Replace

Once you have become honest about your struggles, and you are working to create awareness where you need to change your belief systems, you need to replace the lies with the truth.

This is a constant process. Your brain has literal grooves in it from thinking the same way for so long. It takes time and repetition to change it, to create new grooves. This is where the bigger tests happen.

Replacing the lies with the truth happens when you constantly, with awareness and intention, tell yourself something different. It won't happen by accident. It won't happen by itself. It takes work. Especially when you are struggling with a lie, that is when you need to tell yourself the truth.

Journal section:

#4 Forgive

Forgiveness is often pure choice. It rarely has anything to do with feelings. In fact, you may still feel anger and hatred. But in the middle of feeling angry and hateful, the choice to forgive has the power to break those chains. Only Jesus has the power to help you to choose forgiveness through heated emotions.

Journal section:

Who do I need to forgive?

For what do I need to forgive?

CHAPTER 6
RELIGION VS. RELATIONSHIP: DRESSING UP YOUR FEMININITY

One of the first things that I learned how to sew as a girl was a dress. The dress had to be a specific pattern. It had to reach my ankles in length. The sleeves had to reach at least to my elbows, preferably covering my elbows. The neckline had to come all the way up to my neck. The dress had to be the same style as what every other girl in our church wore. No bright colors, no bold prints, no sheer fabric.

Religion reduces modesty to a set of rules, specifically for how to appear outwardly. Modesty has much more to do with your heart than it has to do with pieces of clothing. Modesty requires you to put your heart in the right place, first. Religion did not allow me to put my heart in the right place. I felt trapped. I couldn't let God lead me in my choices. I was at the mercy of the church leaders.

(Note: I am not saying that church leaders are wrong. There is a vast difference between leaders who control their people vs. leaders who encourage people to listen to God's voice. God's voice comes through leaders who are listening to him.)

129

I was taught that if I was wearing long dresses, my Christianity was established. To even think of wearing something different meant I was on rocky ground.

But it didn't stop me from questioning, in secret.

In my journal, I wrote:

"Can culture hinder our knowledge of Jesus? Why is it so hard to think of breaking away from it? Does it have to define who I am and what I do? Everything is decided for me, how I look, what I say, the lifestyle."

"I think I am an insincere Mennonite."

"I feel like a rebel. I know that everyone would be disappointed in those choices. [the choices I was considering] *But they would be disappointed if they knew it is in my heart already. I feel like I'm playing around with God. I'm not involved wholeheartedly in giving my all for His church. More and more I feel separate from everyone else, because in my heart, I am not where they are. I want something different, I want something more, I want something far more grand and glorious and powerful to give myself to."*

I am not sharing such a personal journey to slam anyone. The church I was part of tried their best to serve God. They did the best they knew. But I also knew that I was responsible for myself, no matter what it looked like or how much it hurt people around me. I had to make my own choices in the end. My choices were not about people. My choices were about my own heart and my own relationship with God.

In the eyes of everyone I knew, I walked away from God. But in my heart, I was finally at home in God. Making outward, visible changes is hard, but there is freedom when you are doing it as a result of the work of God in your heart.

And that is where it all starts.

What Does God See?

1 Peter 3:3-4 says, "Don't be concerned about the outward beauty of fancy hairstyles, expensive jewelry, or beautiful clothes. You should clothe yourselves instead with the beauty that comes from within, the unfading beauty of a gentle and quiet spirit, which is so precious to God."

I always wondered if God cares about what I look like. What matters to him? What does he see that I don't see?

When Samuel was sent by God to anoint one of Jesse's sons to be king, he didn't know which one it would be. The firstborn son (the most likely choice) walked in front of Samuel. Samuel looked at him and thought that he was destined to be the next king.

"But the Lord said to Samuel, 'Don't judge by his appearance or height, for I have rejected him. The Lord doesn't see things the way you see them. People judge by outward appearance, but the Lord looks at the heart.'" (1 Samuel 16:7)

Samuel viewed every son of Jesse that was present, but not one of them was God's chosen king. Samuel asked Jesse if he had any more sons. "'There is still the youngest,' Jesse replied. 'But he's out in the fields watching the sheep and goats.'" (v. 11)

Samuel wanted to see this youngest son, so Jesse sent for him. "He was dark and handsome, with beautiful eyes. And the Lord said, 'This is the one; anoint him.' So as David stood there among his brothers, Samuel took the flask of olive oil he had brought and anointed David with the oil. And the Spirit of the Lord came powerfully upon David from that day on." (v. 12-13)

The extent of human vision is what we possess of our own ability. The things God chooses to reveal to us is his gift of spiritual revelation. Only God can give us spiritual vision. Without him, our spiritual eyes are blind. God, on the other hand, is eternal. He possesses no limits whatsoever. He has no blindness. He has no sin to blemish his vision.

1 John 1:1-7 says, "We proclaim to you the one who existed from the beginning, whom we have heard and seen. We saw him with our own eyes and touched him with our own hands. He is the Word of life. This one who is life itself was revealed to us, and we have seen him. And now we testify and proclaim to you that he is the one who is eternal life. He was with the Father, and then he was revealed to us. We proclaim to you what we ourselves have actually seen and heard so that you may have fellowship with us. And our fellowship is with the Father and with his Son, Jesus Christ. We are writing these things so that you may fully share our joy. This is the message we heard from Jesus and now declare to you: God is light, and there is no darkness in him at all. So we are lying if we say we have fellowship with God but go on living in spiritual darkness; we are not practicing the truth. But if we are living in the light, as God is in the light, then we have fellowship with each other, and the blood of Jesus, his Son, cleanses us from all sin."

John had seen Jesus with his physical eyes. He knew that Jesus was real, but he wanted others to know too, those who didn't have the opportunity to see Jesus. So, he wrote about the way to know Jesus in your heart.

Spoiler alert: It's not about knowing a bunch of rules. It's about practicing the presence of God by listening to his voice and then doing what he says. God alone possesses the ability to see my heart. He is the only one who can cure my spiritual blindness. He does this by showing me who he is. Have I seen him? Has he been revealed to me?

The real test of modesty is in the fruitfulness of my heart. The one who has truly seen Jesus is the one who bears his fruit. The only way that I can see the way that God sees is to turn my focus onto Jesus. I cannot be modest without him. No amount of covering my body will be sufficient righteousness for him, without him.

Religion Vs. Relationship

David's older brothers were all likely good kids. After all, they were the ones invited to be chosen as the next king! David wasn't even invited to witness the event! But God saw the jealousy of the brothers. He saw their inner hearts. He saw the patience of David, his practicing and improving of skills, his faithfulness in his work. Only God saw David's growth, out on the hillside, watching sheep.

David knew the value of being faithful while being unseen. He was faithful in the hidden places. He knew that before he could be elevated, he had to choose to be seen as lesser. And he was seen as lesser. His family did not appreciate him. But because he chose humility, he was the next chosen king!

Jesus chose this same path of humility, leading to elevation.

Philippians 2:6-11 says, "Though he was God, he did not think of equality with God as something to cling to. Instead, he gave up his divine privileges; he took the humble position of a slave and was born as a human being. When he appeared in human form, he humbled himself in obedience to God and died a criminal's death on a cross. Therefore, God elevated him to the place of highest honor and gave him the name above all other names, that at the name of Jesus every knee should bow, in heaven and on earth and under the earth, and every tongue confess that Jesus Christ is Lord, to the glory of God the Father."

It is easy enough to say with my mouth that Jesus Christ is the Lord of my life, but it is not until my lifestyle and daily habits reflect the attitude of the cross that those words will carry any weight. The cross is not a one-time event. The cross is my daily choice. It is a life built on the cross that results in resurrection power. It is a life marked by death that glows with the glory of God.

It is not by doing good things in the eyes of others that Jesus will honor us. It is obedience in the secret place.

That is religion versus relationship. Religion equals following a set of rules; relationship means creating an open heart for God to dwell. Both religion and relationship have a tremendous effect on outward appearances. Religion places the focus outward, but relationship starts on the inside.

Colossians 3:12-15 says, "Since God chose you to be the holy people he loves, you must clothe yourselves with tenderhearted mercy, kindness, humility, gentleness, and patience. Make allowance for each other's faults, and forgive anyone who offends you. Remember, the Lord forgave you, so you must forgive others. Above all, clothe yourselves with love, which binds us all together in perfect harmony. And let the peace that comes from Christ rule in your hearts. For as members of one body you are called to live in peace. And always be thankful."

Religion is a cheap version of the life God calls us to live. It does not require character and heart changes for me to be religious.

Relationship is the real thing. Follow Jesus and allow him to change your heart. It's not natural for me to be merciful, kind, humble, gentle, and patient. I do not easily forgive or allow space for others to be imperfect. I do not easily choose to love.

Yet this is the path we are called to walk.

Living in the light means having a relationship with God where my heart is completely exposed and vulnerable to him. Instead of trying to hide fear, shame, insecurity, bitterness, we choose to allow him into the secret spaces. If we do not choose to open up to God, we are living in darkness. If we do not choose to give up our secret selfishness, we are living in darkness. God will never shame us when we go to him and tell him our secrets. He has provided the blood of Jesus to wash the darkness away. He will show you grace and forgiveness as you seek to change and grow.

Living in the light is the only way I can properly see, inside. It's the only way my blind spots are removed. It starts with our map:

Reveal the lies (be honest)

Release the lies (bind the lies)

Replace with truth

Restore (forgive)

Living in the light does affect my outward appearance. It does make a difference in how I look. But unlike religion, the focus is not necessarily about actual clothing. My clothing choices are not what God will target first. He will first target my heart, and the clothing choices will flow from that place.

Proverbs 31:25-26 says, "She is clothed with strength and dignity, and she laughs without fear of the future. When she speaks, her words are wise, and she gives instructions with kindness."

What does it mean to be clothed with strength and dignity?

I can be dressed outwardly with beautiful clothes, but inside, my heart can be filled with jealousy, shame, or fear. God calls me to align my heart with my outward choices. Why? Because what is in my heart will always affect my behavior, no matter what kind of clothes I am wearing.

God values forgiveness, love, peace, gratitude, and mercy in my heart far above a specific way of dressing. Strength and dignity are character qualities that will reveal what is in my heart through how I behave. A strong, dignified woman will not be a pushover to fear, gossip, or shame. She will use her life to bless others and to bring life to everyone around her.

A strong, dignified woman will choose to honor others with every area of her life. She will develop refined manners. Her interactions with others will be thoughtful, intentional, and loving. Anxiety has no place in her life - past, present, or future. Being a restful person because the Prince of Peace rules your heart is much more important than appearing "right" outwardly.

God does not require you to look put-together before you come to him. All he wants is your heart. Once your heart has been cleansed and filled with light, your appearance will become aligned to the light of Jesus.

The Communication of Outward Appearance

1 Timothy 2:9-10 says, "And I want women to be modest in their appearance. They should wear decent and appropriate clothing and not draw attention to themselves by the way they fix their hair or by wearing gold or pearls or expensive clothes. For women who claim to be devoted to God should make themselves attractive by the good things they do."

Again, 1 Peter 3:3-4 says, "Don't be concerned about the outward beauty of fancy hairstyles, expensive jewelry, or beautiful clothes. You should clothe yourselves instead with the beauty that comes from within, the unfading beauty of a gentle and quiet spirit, which is so precious to God."

Religion says that these verses are telling us not to decorate our hair or wear jewelry or fancy clothes. But what does relationship say?

It's not telling me that it's wrong to wear certain clothes! It's saying that on the inside, I need to die so that through my life, Jesus shines in his beauty. It's not saying that hair or jewelry is inconsistent with modesty. It's saying that when my heart is captivated with myself, I will be immodest no matter how I appear. It's saying that love for myself is inconsistent with modesty. When I love myself more than I love Jesus, I will use hair, clothes, jewelry, and makeup to draw attention to myself. When I love Jesus more than myself, I will use these things as tools to show his beautiful, glorious presence in my heart.

Paul and Peter are making connections between your heart and your body. They are addressing motives and desires rather than outfits. The only way that beauty is wrong is if it conflicts with God's glory. How important is your appearance to you? If it determines your security, that is where it is out of place.

You are meant to sparkle, but your sparkle shouldn't define you. Rather, your sparkle should flow from the joy of the Lord overflowing in your heart. The Holy Spirit should have permission to give your face a holy glow, no matter if you are wearing makeup or not.

Even if you feel tired, impatient, unloving, unkind, unhappy, you can choose to clothe yourself in rest, patience, love, kindness, joy. You aren't a victim to your selfishness, because the Holy Spirit gives you the power to choose to die to yourself.

Galatians 5:22 says, "The Holy Spirit produces this kind of fruit in our lives: love, joy, peace, patience, kindness, goodness, faithfulness, gentleness, and self-control. There is no law against these things!"

This is where true beauty, holiness, and modesty comes from - a relationship in which the Spirit of God is free to move! If your motive in your appearance is to glorify him, he will have the power to direct you in how to appear.

The kind of clothes that are most important to God, that he sees first, are the clothes of love, patience, kindness. Each day, we should wake up and inwardly dress ourselves with these character qualities, by putting ourselves under the authority of the Holy Spirit.

Inner Glow Becomes Outer Glow Up

The inner glow of the Holy Spirit becomes a reflection on your face. Your face shows what is inside of you, especially your eyes. The inner glow becomes an outer glow up. What people will notice about you, more than a piece of clothing, is the expression on your face, because your face is where you interact with them. Your face can make someone feel judged and condemned or loved and accepted.

The inner glow becomes practical on the outside. The manifestation of kindness, love, and joy is practical.

You can dress in a way that highlights specific character qualities that God is forming in you. Just as a room is painted to give it a certain feel, certain colors, styles, and outfits will give you a specific "feel" to others. Think of your outward appearance as a way to communicate with others what you want them to feel about your character. Modesty is all about the attitudes and motivations of your heart. Your motivation shows itself outwardly, by your behavior.

When I asked my husband what is attractive in a woman, he said that it is more than half about what kind of personality she has. In other words, a woman who smiles and radiates genuine joy and love is much more attractive than a woman who is insecure and afraid to be herself.

Your personality is worn on your face.

I had to learn some practical things about my face in order to better reflect who I am as a woman.

I had to learn my face shape. My face shape determines what kind of glasses I should wear, how to accent certain parts of my face with makeup, and what kind of hairstyles look best on me. I learned that bangs are an excellent choice for me. (This is specific to your face and what will make you appear the most presentable. What works for me may not work for someone else with a different face shape.)

I also had to learn how to hold my face. I became aware of my tendency to hold my face in a certain way when I wasn't talking or smiling. My unintentional expression was unattractive. I held my face in a sort of frown. I learned that if I would practice holding the muscles in my mouth upward, it would make me appear to be a restful, joyful person. Over time, it became my natural expression.

With my face shape, I also learned that my eyebrows look best if they are kept trimmed in a certain shape.

As I learned how to translate my inner glow outwardly, I also developed a habit of smiling often. Do not underestimate the power of a genuine smile. Do not fake a smile. Let it be an overflow of your inner joy and radiance.

The way that you speak is also tremendously important. Your voice speaks volumes about who you are, inside (no pun intended). Your tongue has the power to build or destroy relationships, depending on whether you choose love or jealousy to rule your heart. What content does my tongue engage in on a consistent basis? Does my tongue control conversations or do I allow space to hear others? How well do I listen? Do I speak too loudly or too softly? Do I yell when I should be soft? Do I speak too quietly when I should be bold? What is the undercurrent of my words? What am I communicating beneath my words?

As you drink in from the abundance of God's love, it will naturally overflow and become a place where people are attracted to. It's not about you. It's not about me. It's about HIM.

Exercises

#1 Reveal

What am I feeling right now?

Why am I feeling this way?

What lies am I believing?

Where do the lies come from?

What am I allowing to control my mind?

What shuts me down?

What causes me to stop dreaming?

What is my biggest fear?

#2 Release

This step is all about creating awareness. When you have lived for a long time with habits of thinking a certain way, it requires a commitment to daily train yourself to think differently-not an easy task. Catch yourself in the act of believing a lie. Don't let the lie go. It's easy to slip, especially in the beginning. The beginning is the hardest.

Find the Scripture verses that speak to the lies in your head. I have often turned on audio Scriptures when Satan was fighting to shut my mouth. Not today, Satan!

Speak those verses out loud. The louder, the better. I remember many car drives when I would use the time to really get the words out with volume. Spoken words shift the atmosphere drastically. Satan hears what you say. Say it as though you believe it! Take authority over your mind.

Journal section:

Bible verses:

#3 Replace

Once you have become honest about your struggles, and you are working to create awareness where you need to change your belief systems, you need to replace the lies with the truth.

This is a constant process. Your brain has literal grooves in it from thinking the same way for so long. It takes time and repetition to change it, to create new grooves. This is where the bigger tests happen.

Replacing the lies with the truth happens when you constantly, with awareness and intention, tell yourself something different. It won't happen by accident. It won't happen by itself. It takes work. Especially when you are struggling with a lie, that is when you need to tell yourself the truth.

Journal section:

#4 Forgive

Forgiveness is often pure choice. It rarely has anything to do with feelings. In fact, you may still feel anger and hatred. But in the middle of feeling angry and hateful, the choice to forgive has the power to break those chains. Only Jesus has the power to help you to choose forgiveness through heated emotions.

Journal section:

Who do I need to forgive?

For what do I need to forgive?

CHAPTER 7
DEVELOPING A DISCERNING HEART: HOW TO MAKE YOUR HOME A SANCTUARY

What really makes a home feel like home? Who or what gives you that sweet sense of belonging? Does it really matter what your home looks like? Is "home" a place, a feeling, or a person?

I always dreamed of having my own house. I looked forward to the day I could take care of a house for people I loved. But I didn't want only a physically clean house; I wanted a spiritually clean atmosphere and a loving environment where others felt welcome. I wanted to create a beautiful, hospitable environment.

The question I had was, how?

When I got married, I didn't know how to make my dream real life, but I wanted to learn. It took time and experience, but through a lot of trial and error, I learned a lot.

Even if you don't have your own house, you have a living space. Everyone makes choices about how to live and behave in their space. Everyone invites a certain atmosphere into their space. It is each person's job to examine exactly what she allows to dwell in that space.

That "space" or "house" looks different for everyone. But certain elements contribute a lot to that homey feeling. Having a clean house, with good food, and a family you love is what most people think of in a home. Things and people are what bring the "home" into a physical space.

But there is another level than the physical space. I consider my house homier when the people I love are there with me. But I have come to understand another level of home and how to create a holy atmosphere anywhere I go.

The people who live in a specific house contribute in very specific ways to what kind of atmosphere is in the house. But I'm not responsible for the choices of the person next to me. I am responsible for my choices. I can choose to live a certain way regardless of someone else. My lifestyle exercises more influence over others than I realize. It takes a lot of effort. Patience. Hard work. Discipline. But it's worth it. The more that you discipline yourself, the more reward you will get. Discipline comes with purpose.

But I'm getting ahead of myself.

The Way to Worship

Romans 12:1-2 says, "And so, dear brothers and sisters, I plead with you to give your bodies to God because of all he has done for you. Let them be a living and holy sacrifice - the kind he will find acceptable. This is truly the way to worship him. Don't copy the behavior and customs of this world, but let God transform you into a new person by changing the way you think. Then you will learn to know God's will for you, which is good and pleasing and perfect."

There is more to our physical bodies than our physical bodies. We have a soul, mind, and spirit. We have desires, dreams, motives, thoughts. We are always gravitating toward something. Our behavior comes out of our hearts - where we desire, dream, think. What we want most and think about most is what we worship. Our behavior affects our environment. If we want to change our environment, we need to dig down and discover what is in our hearts.

This is why taking personal responsibility is so important. I can't change someone else's heart. But I can choose to change myself through the power of the Holy Spirit.

So, the question is - Where am I gravitating towards?

What does my behavior say about what is in my heart?

A living space is where my heart is expressed. My behavior will show whether I am contributing well to the atmosphere or if I am bringing negativity.

We all carry baggage. We all have had experiences that shaped us, that gave us a lens through which we view life. If we have not dealt with past experiences that we have allowed to define us, we will live out of the identities assigned to us by those experiences.

This is why we need to follow our map:

Reveal the lies.

Release the lies.

Replace with truth.

Restore (forgive)

A holy atmosphere is created by a person who loves Jesus. Jesus in us has the power to change everything around us. He has the power to change hearts.

Why is the spiritual atmosphere in your home important?

- As believers, nothing in our lives is neutral. We must filter our every action, thought, word, through the Scriptures and the Holy Spirit.
- We are called to glorify God in every area.
- Our homes are given to us by God. Taking care of every area, including the spiritual atmosphere of your home, is being good stewards of God's gifts to us.
- It reflects the state of our hearts. We can clean our houses all day and still have a dirty house because we are ungrateful, anxious, or bitter.

- It affects relationships. If relationships are weak, it means that love is missing from the atmosphere. People know when they are in a place where they will be either judged or loved, criticized or welcomed, *especially kids.*

When my husband and I got married, we moved into an apartment. This apartment had an unclean atmosphere. There were times when I was fighting through things in my life, and I had to face demonic activity as a result. For example, one time, I was worshiping on my piano in order to reach breakthrough in a specific struggle, and I did reach breakthrough. After I stopped playing, I went to bed, and the light that was hanging above the piano, with no warning, fell down! It had never happened before. I could sense I had reached a new level, and Satan was throwing a fit!

But that apartment had more demonic activity in it than was warranted by our spiritual breakthroughs. (In fact, spiritual breakthroughs should result in demons fleeing!) Almost every night, my husband and I prayed against it for hours. It was especially strong in the bedroom closet. One night, the darkness was so potent, that my husband saw demons moving around the bed. We heard cackling laughter. My husband felt the strangest thing - at the foot of the bed, he felt a demon lift the blanket, and he felt heat. That was the worst night of all. We played worship music and prayed until the darkness left.

It was so strange that we concluded a previous tenant must have had some associations there.

We lived in that apartment for a year, and then we moved into a different apartment about ten minutes away. The very first night in the new place, we sensed no demonic activity! The atmosphere in the new place was consistently clear, although we still prayed over it.

I am not sharing this story to scare anyone, but as a testimony to encourage you to fight for the peace of your home.

Most of the time, the demons we faced in the first apartment were not there because of us. They felt like witchcraft level, and we were not involved in anything that would invite them in. Although that was a rather scary year, we learned so many lessons in our marriage because of it. It unified us in the battle. We fought a spiritual war on the turf of our home, and we fought together. Satan was, and is, our common enemy. We were aware that the battle was not against each other. It taught us the importance of having pure hearts. We regularly examined our hearts to ensure we were clear.

1 Corinthians 10

"I don't want you to forget, dear brothers and sisters, about our ancestors in the wilderness long ago. All of them were guided by a cloud that moved ahead of them, and all of them walked through the sea on dry ground. In the cloud and in the sea, all of them were baptized as followers of Moses. All of them ate the same spiritual food, and all of them drank the same spiritual water. For they drank from the spiritual rock that traveled with them, and that rock was Christ. Yet God was not pleased with most of them, and their bodies were scattered in the wilderness. These things happened as a warning to us, so that we would not crave evil things as they did, or worship idols as some of them did. As the Scriptures say, 'The people celebrated with feasting and drinking, and they indulged in pagan revelry.' And we must not engage in sexual immorality as some of them did, causing 23,000 of them to die in one day.

"Nor should we put Christ to the test, as some of them did and then died from snakebites. And don't grumble as some of them did, and then were destroyed by the angel of death. These things happened to them as examples for us. They were written down to warn us who live at the end of the age. If you think you are standing strong, be careful not to fall. The temptations in your life are no different from what others experience. And God is faithful. He will not allow the temptation to be more than you can stand. When you are tempted, he will show you a way out so that you can endure. So, my dear friends, flee from the worship of idols. You are reasonable people. Decide for yourselves if what I am saying is true. When we bless the cup at the Lord's Table, aren't we sharing in the blood of Christ? And when we break the bread, aren't we sharing in the body of Christ? And though we are many, we all eat from one loaf of bread, showing that we are one body. Think about the people of Israel. Weren't they united by eating the sacrifices at the altar?

"What am I trying to say? Am I saying that food offered to idols has some significance, or that idols are real gods? No, not at all. I am saying that these sacrifices are offered to demons, not to God. And I don't want you to participate with demons. You cannot drink from the cup of the Lord and from the cup of demons, too. You cannot eat at the Lord's Table and at the table of demons, too. What? Do we dare to rouse the Lord's jealousy? Do you think we are stronger than he is?

"You say, 'I am allowed to do anything' - but not everything is good for you. You say, 'I am allowed to do anything' - but not everything is beneficial. Don't be concerned for your own good but for the good of others.

"So you may eat any meat that is sold in the marketplace without raising questions of conscience. For 'the earth is the Lord's, and everything in it.'

"If someone who isn't a believer asks you home for dinner, accept the invitation if you want to. Eat whatever is offered to you without raising questions of conscience. (But suppose someone tells you, 'This meat was offered to an idol.' Don't eat it, out of consideration for the conscience of the one who told you. It might not be a matter of conscience for you, but it is for the other person.) For why should my freedom be limited by what someone else thinks? If I can thank God for the food and enjoy it, why should I be condemned for eating it?

"So whether you eat or drink, or whatever you do, do it all for the glory of God. Don't give offense to Jews or Gentiles or the church of God. I, too, try to please everyone in everything I do. I don't just do what is best for me; I do what is best for others so that many may be saved. And you should imitate me, just as I imitate Christ."

Paul highlights the fact that we can't just go to church on Sunday and call ourselves good for the rest of the week. What my life looks like daily matters. What my heart looks like daily matters.

Developing A Discerning Heart: How to Make Your Home A Sanctuary

Paul uses the story of the Israelites to illustrate this. The Israelites were all involved in God's amazing rescue from Egypt. Yet they immediately turned away from God and worshiped idols, engaged in sexual sin, and grumbled. They forgot. They became consumed with their own desires for pleasure and relief from the hardships of the desert.

This is exactly how we are. God has delivered us with the sacrifice of his only Son, and yet, we turn away and secretly engage in our sins again. We forget. We may look "right" on the outside, but inside, we are angry with God for apparently forsaking us. Our hearts are anything but worshipful of God. Our lives become marked by sin and sexual immorality and faithlessness. We doubt God when we should believe.

But God is faithful. He uses these struggles. For the Israelites, it was a warning to us. For us, it is a test of our hearts. Where does our loyalty lie? It will show up in the way that we respond when our hearts are tested. Do we consider God's glory in daily decisions? Do we consider what God thinks about our everyday lives?

The things that I do matter. It is not legalism. It is a desire to obey, to follow my Lord, to carry my cross on the narrow path of love for only him. My body is his temple (1 Corinthians 6:19). My body, including my mind, soul, and spirit. The spiritual side of me is where he makes his temple.

I am God's house of prayer. It is not enough to say that I love Jesus. My lifestyle must prove it. Otherwise, I will be full of noise about God, but I will not be godly.

My behavior opens up doors to invite either heaven or hell into my life. Spiritual realms are activated by my choices. Satan is not ignorant of where my heart is, because he observes my behavior. He knows exactly where to place his arrows of poison.

The way I live does not affect only myself. It affects everyone around me, as well.

The number one question for everything I do is, "Is God pleased?" It's never a fear that God will punish me for displeasing him. It's knowing that he loves me through all my mess, and that his love will not passively observe my mistakes, but actively seek to rescue and restore my heart to his through my failures. His love will expose the areas where I need to grow.

Discernment is the Key

1 Corinthians 14:33 says, "For God is not a God of disorder but of peace."

Developing A Discerning Heart: How to Make Your Home A Sanctuary

1 Peter 1:13-16 says, "So think clearly and exercise self-control. Look forward to the gracious salvation that will come to you when Jesus Christ is revealed to the world. So you must live as God's obedient children. Don't slip back into your old ways of living to satisfy your own desires. You didn't know any better then. But now you must be holy in everything you do, just as God who chose you is holy. For the Scriptures say, 'You must be holy because I am holy.'"

If you want your personal space to be full of joy, love, hope, peace, you need to discern. Exercise your senses. If your spirit feels unclear, press into the problem in prayer until something shifts.

In the 1 Corinthians 10 chapter, Paul says, "Decide for yourselves if what I am saying is true." I am not a victim. I can choose to believe something is true or untrue, but it will show up in the way that I live. Discernment will level up my lifestyle, because it will elevate my belief system.

Temptations (aka struggles) will give me a window into where my beliefs need to be adjusted. God doesn't provide escapes. He provides wisdom. He is the standard of beliefs and where my heart fails to measure up is where change needs to happen. He is where discernment comes from. How do I know how to discern if I don't know God? I can't. It takes his wisdom. It takes his truth.

James 1:2-8 says, "Dear brothers and sisters, when troubles come your way, consider it an opportunity for great joy. For you know that when your faith is tested, your endurance has a chance to grow. So let it grow, for when your endurance is fully developed, you will be perfect and complete, needing nothing. If you need wisdom, ask our generous God, and he will give it to you. He will not rebuke you for asking. But when you ask him, be sure that your faith is in God alone. Do not waver, for a person with divided loyalty is as unsettled as a wave of the sea that is blown and tossed by the wind. Such people should not expect to receive anything from the Lord. Their loyalty is divided between God and the world, and they are unstable in everything they do."

How do I get discernment? Ask God for wisdom.

When I ask God for something, he doesn't give me what I ask for unless he knows that my heart is pure. If he sees that my heart is really desiring my request for myself, he won't give it to me, at least not in the way that I want. Wisdom is not my desires realized as truth. Wisdom is God's desires realized as truth. I won't be able to receive wisdom until I give up my desires.

The First Step to Practicing Discernment

Developing A Discerning Heart: How to Make Your Home A Sanctuary

Hebrews 5 :11-14 says, "There is much more we would like to say about this, but it is difficult to explain, especially since you are spiritually dull and don't seem to listen. You have been believers so long now that you ought to be teaching others. Instead, you need someone to teach you again the basic things about God's word. You are like babies who need milk and cannot eat solid food. For someone who lives on milk is still an infant and doesn't know how to do what is right. Solid food is for those who are mature, who through training have the skill to recognize the difference between right and wrong."

The first step to practicing discernment is the development of my spiritual ears. If I am not listening to God's voice, I am listening to a voice of lies. I must develop sensitivity to the still, small voice of the Holy Spirit. This is the difference between milk and solid food: willingness to listen and obey. The more I obey, the stronger the voice of wisdom becomes (solid food). But if I push it away, the less I will hear it (milk). Eventually the milk will dry up and there will be no spiritual sustenance.

Solid food also implies that I am strong enough (with God but without people) to lead myself into God's truth. Milk is like having someone spoon-feed me God's truth. A brand-new believer needs milk, but their leader should be teaching them how to depend on God from day one. Yes, we all need godly people to help and lead and encourage us, but the point is that God is my strength and refuge, and people are tools in his hands to point us to him.

Someone who lives on milk is much more likely to swallow whatever is given to them, rather than testing it out (discern). My one-year-old son Liam is a perfect example of this. He loves milk, but he will put anything into his mouth. He will eat dirt, or chew on rocks. I am constantly finding new things in his mouth. If I haven't swept the floor recently, he will pick up any little piece of food or dirt that has fallen on the floor, and yes, eat it. As he gets older, he will learn how to discern between a rock and real food.

The Second Step in Practicing Discernment

The second step in practicing discernment is obedience.

James 1:22-25 says, "But don't just listen to God's word. You must do what it says. Otherwise, you are only fooling yourselves. For if you listen to the word and don't obey, it is like glancing at your face in a mirror. You see yourself, walk away, and forget what you look like. But if you look carefully into the perfect law that sets you free, and if you do what it says and don't forget what you heard, then God will bless you for doing it."

Hearing without doing is a fruitless life. Partial obedience is not true obedience.

Developing A Discerning Heart: How to Make Your Home A Sanctuary

Revelation 3:15-20 says, "I know all the things you do, that you are neither hot nor cold. I wish that you were one or the other! But since you are like lukewarm water, neither hot nor cold, I will spit you out of my mouth! You say, 'I am rich. I have everything I want. I don't need a thing! And you don't realize that you are wretched and miserable and poor and blind and naked. So I advise you to buy gold from me - gold that has been purified by fire. Then you will be rich. Also buy white garments from me so you will not be shamed by your nakedness, and ointment for your eyes so you will be able to see. I correct and discipline everyone I love. So be diligent and turn from your indifference. Look! I stand at the door and knock. If you hear my voice and open the door, I will come in, and we will share a meal together as friends."

In order to develop my ear to hear and my life to obey, I must develop awareness around where I am foolish and disobedient. When I am made aware by the Holy Spirit of something in my life that is ungodly, how quick am I to repent and make changes? The gap between hearing and doing should be constantly shrinking. I should never wait to obey. That is a sign of coldness, or worse, lukewarmness.

My cup of coffee is usually cold by the time I finish it. I am a busy mom. I pour it hot, of course, but I am busy doing things as I drink it. I am also not a fast drinker. So I often have to either microwave my coffee, or force myself to swallow lukewarm coffee.

If I was married to someone who said with his mouth that he loved me, but did nothing to show me his love, I would feel cheated. It would feel like drinking that lukewarm coffee. I would not feel loved. How much of my life communicates this lack of love for God?

The Third Step to Practicing Discernment

The third step to practicing discernment is to examine my life, based on the wisdom God gives to me as I hear and obey.

What is my appetite? What do I hunger for? What fruit does my life show that I am hungry for God? How quick am I to obey?

1 John 2:15-17 says, "Do not love this world nor the things it offers you, for when you love the world, you do not have the love of the Father in you. For the world offers only a craving for physical pleasure, a craving for everything we see, and pride in our achievements and possessions. These are not from the Father, but are from this world. And this world is fading away, along with everything that people crave. But anyone who does what pleases God will live forever."

Is my life "sharing a meal together with God" or is it consumption of my desires?

The Fourth Step to Practicing Discernment

The fourth step is to repent and to make changes as quickly as possible.

As I am quick to hear, obey, examine, and repent, it will result in a deep, Spirit-filled vision. I will have clarity. My senses will become strong as they are exercised to feel the atmosphere.

It's all about the replacement. Repentance must result in replacement. I must replace my worldly appetite with hunger for God. I must replace the foolishness of my flesh with the wisdom of God. I must replace the fear of man with the fear of God.

Practicing discernment is very practical in its expression. As Paul said in 1 Corinthians 10, we cannot drink from the cup of the Lord and of demons. God is jealous for that center stage of my heart. He will not share. When I take God seriously, I will treat all my life and activities with a discerning heart.

The world has an agenda, because its king is Satan. There are many things that the world engages in that, as believers, we cannot, because its agenda is to tear down God's kingdom. But it is so subtle that it requires daily Spirit-filled wisdom to know the difference.

Regularly feeding on the word of God is vital to discernment. If anything in my life contradicts God's word, it must be changed. It is the daily hearing of God's word and the practical walking it out that will create a flow of the Holy Spirit and his still, small voice of wisdom, guiding my steps.

Philippians 4:8-9 says, "Fix your thoughts on what is true, and honorable, and right, and pure, and lovely, and admirable. Think about things that are excellent and worthy of praise. Keep putting into practice all you learned and received from me - everything you heard from me and saw me doing. Then the God of peace will be with you."

It's all about trajectory. I have felt discouraged many times because I felt like I haven't "arrived" yet. But it's not about arriving right now, because eternity is my destiny. Right now, today, is my life on an upward trending point of growth, or is it trending downwards, into the world's gutter of filth and foolishness? It's one step upwards at a time that the prize is won.

Philippians 3:12-14 says, "I don't mean to say that I have already achieved these things or that I have already reached perfection. But I press on to possess that perfection for which Christ Jesus first possessed me. No, dear brothers and sisters, I have not achieved it, but I focus on this one thing: Forgetting the past and looking forward to what lies ahead, I press on to reach the end of the race and receive the heavenly prize for which God, through Christ Jesus, is calling us."

These are some practical ways we felt God called us to clean the atmosphere in our home.

- Be mindful of movies and music. This is not a legalistic thing of what is right and what is wrong. It's "What is leading my heart away from God by filling my life with noise and distraction?"
- Prayer walk the house. Satan wants to camp in your house. He will try to find a foothold somehow, somewhere. Pray your way to freedom. Prayer is one of the most powerful tools for cleansing the atmosphere. Pray Until Something Happens. PUSH through the blocks. Prayer is where you gain clarity and receive wisdom. Prayer is where you receive direction. Prayer is where God moves!
- Do a fast from anything you sense is not clear. If God reveals to you an activity that you engage in that is not godly, do a fast. See what happens. Fasting is also where God moves.
- Anoint the walls of your house with oil. It is a powerful, visible sign of God's presence.
- Play worship music. Music is another very powerful tool that can usher in God's presence and cleanse the atmosphere. Worship is a weapon. Use it.

- Be mindful of words. Speaking words of discouragement, doubt, or fear causes that kind of an environment. Speaking words of life creates life! You will need to examine your heart and see where your words are coming from. (Matthew 7:17-19, James 3:7-12, Luke 6:45)
- Speak God's word over your house, your life, finances, marriage, kids, health. Claim his promises. Press in to receive what he's promised you. He doesn't give his abundant blessings where they will be wasted. Live a life that is worthy of blessing.
- Keep a clear heart. Proverbs 4:23 says, "Guard your heart above all else, for it determines the course of your life."
- Forgive. This is one of the biggest obstacles to moving forward, if you are unwilling to forgive. Forgiveness will break down walls and bring fresh, new life into dead, dry hearts. Ask God to teach you how to forgive. Forgiveness is a God-thing.

Developing A Discerning Heart: How to Make Your Home A Sanctuary

Lay out all your cards on the table (where you spend your time, thought processes, behaviors, etc.) and ask the Lord if there are any open doors to the enemy. You can't participate in darkness, break it off, and continue to be involved in dark things. You must stop the involvement in dark things after it is broken off. Continued intentional involvement in darkness after breaking off the darkness will only invite it into your life in a stronger way. This is why replacement of God's light after breaking it off is important.

In the process of bringing the Lord into your living space, it is normal for Satan to attack where he sees light coming in. But it is important to recognize that attacks are not negative or discouraging. Attacks are a sign of growth and health. It is our response to attacks that matters. It means that God is pushing new growth into old places. Do not roll over and play dead when the enemy attacks. Often, the hardest things happen right before big breakthroughs. The best thing to do is to keep doing what you've been doing, the things you did that caused Satan to take notice. It means your life is becoming effective and catching fire.

The goal in life is to know God and to make him known. Who is God? God is love. Love and fear are opposite, so when fear attacks, it means that there are areas of your life that need love. The Lord is simply taking you to the next level of love.

Exercises

#1 Reveal

What am I feeling right now?

Why am I feeling this way?

What lies am I believing?

Where do the lies come from?

What am I allowing to control my mind?

What shuts me down?

What causes me to stop dreaming?

What is my biggest fear?

#2 Release

This step is all about creating awareness. When you have lived for a long time with habits of thinking a certain way, it requires a commitment to daily train yourself to think differently-not an easy task. Catch yourself in the act of believing a lie. Don't let the lie go. It's easy to slip, especially in the beginning. The beginning is the hardest.

Find the Scripture verses that speak to the lies in your head. I have often turned on audio Scriptures when Satan was fighting to shut my mouth. Not today, Satan!

Speak those verses out loud. The louder, the better. I remember many car drives when I would use the time to really get the words out with volume. Spoken words shift the atmosphere drastically. Satan hears what you say. Say it as though you believe it! Take authority over your mind.

Journal section:

Bible verses:

#3 Replace

Once you have become honest about your struggles, and you are working to create awareness where you need to change your belief systems, you need to replace the lies with the truth.

This is a constant process. Your brain has literal grooves in it from thinking the same way for so long. It takes time and repetition to change it, to create new grooves. This is where the bigger tests happen.

Replacing the lies with the truth happens when you constantly, with awareness and intention, tell yourself something different. It won't happen by accident. It won't happen by itself. It takes work. Especially when you are struggling with a lie, that is when you need to tell yourself the truth.

Journal section:

#4 Forgive

Forgiveness is often pure choice. It rarely has anything to do with feelings. In fact, you may still feel anger and hatred. But in the middle of feeling angry and hateful, the choice to forgive has the power to break those chains. Only Jesus has the power to help you to choose forgiveness through heated emotions.

Journal section:

Who do I need to forgive?

For what do I need to forgive?

CHAPTER 8

OVERCOMING THE VICTIM MINDSET: HOW TO LOVE OTHERS WELL

did not grow up with people skills. Because I had been hurt, I saw people as a threat to my safety. Therefore, I had very few friends.

Not only did I lack friendships, I lacked connection with my family, too. I am not blaming any of my family members. They all did the best they could with the circumstances we had. But the reality is that I had a lot of fear, shame, and self-hatred, and as a child, I needed to feel safe somehow. My solution was to put up walls. The walls I put up blocked off even my own family. I learned that if I wanted to feel safe, I couldn't talk, because talking made me heard, and that made me vulnerable to pain.

So, I talked as little as possible, in the quietest voice I could find, and pretended that everything was fine in my little world hidden behind the walls.

I was very good at pretending. But inside, I knew that I was hiding my real self, and I knew that I must have a voice in there somewhere.

This has been one of the most difficult lies for me to overcome: "You're quiet."

Words hold power. Proverbs 18:21 says, "The tongue can bring death or life."

The words "You're quiet" were spoken over me, and each time, I felt suffocated, stifled, choked to death. I was expected to say nothing. My voice was unheard. I felt so powerless. I felt like I had no identity. No one believed I could talk.

Finding my voice has been my biggest struggle as an adult. I cried the first time I was told that I wasn't quiet.

Let There Be Light in My Suffering

Genesis 1:1-4 says, "In the beginning God created the heavens and the earth. The earth was formless and empty, and darkness covered the deep waters. And the Spirit of God was hovering over the surface of the waters. Then God said, 'Let there be light,' and there was light. And God saw that the light was good."

Psalm 139:7-16 says, "I can never escape from your Spirit! I can never get away from your presence! If I go up to heaven, you are there; if I go down to the grave, you are there. If I ride the wings of the morning, if I dwell by the farthest oceans, even there your hand will guide me, and your strength will support me. I could ask the darkness to hide me and the light around me to become night - but even in darkness I cannot hide from you. To you the night shines as bright as day. Darkness and light are the same to you. You made all the delicate, inner parts of my body and knit me together in my mother's womb. Thank you for making me so wonderfully complex! Your workmanship is marvelous - how well I know it. You watched me as I was being formed in utter seclusion, as I was woven together in the dark of the womb. You saw me before I was born."

In Genesis 1, God created the light, knowing that the darkness of sin would soon enter his beautiful creation. Genesis 3:8 says that Adam and Eve hid from God. Was it that God had failed them? No, it was that Adam and Eve had broken God's command.

Because of sin, we all try to hide from God, just as I hid my real self as a child. But God works in the darkness. He doesn't need light, because he is Light.

It is abundantly clear that there is a lot of hurt in this world. It is obvious that hurt people hurt others, whether it is intentional or not. Many people blame God for their pain. I did, for years. But God does not hurt you. God is not to blame for all the hurt in this world.

Whenever we get hurt, we want to place the blame somewhere. We often blame others or God (or both). If God is all-powerful, why does he not stop the pain?

The answers are not easy.

God does not do my will. Jesus prayed before he was betrayed, "Father, if you are willing, please take this cup of suffering away from me. Yet I want your will to be done, not mine." (Luke 22:42) Luke 23:34 says, "Jesus said, 'Father, forgive them, for they don't know what they are doing.'"

God is not responsible for my suffering. He uses pain to teach me lessons. He heals my pain with his love. What would a painless life do to me? How would I grow without pain?

Pain gives me a responsibility to suffer well. Pain is not what ultimately matters; it is my response to it that matters.

My perception of God as either a perpetrator of pain or a healer of pain colors my interactions with others. I had to learn to not reflect on God the lack of character qualities I saw in people who hurt me. I had to learn where my responsibility began. Where others had failed me, God was still faithful. And because of his faithfulness, I found hope again.

In that place, I learned to not find my identity in a label. Rather than claiming my safety as an "introvert" and giving myself an excuse to keep hiding, I had to push myself out of my comfort zone and do hard things that aligned myself with the identity of a daughter of God.

179

(Note: Being an introvert is not wrong. Using it as an excuse to not obey God is wrong.)

Learning how to love others well is not optional for a child of God. If we claim to love God, we must love others.

Matthew 22:37-39 says, "'You must love the Lord your God with all your heart, all your soul, and all your mind.' This is the first and greatest commandment. A second is equally important: 'Love your neighbor as yourself.'"

John 13:34-35 says, "So now I am giving you a new commandment: Love each other. Just as I have loved you, you should love each other. Your love for one another will prove to the world that you are my disciples."

I understand that there are many people who have grown up in healthy families and who do not struggle to talk. But that is not my story, and the words I speak now I have fought many battles for.

Proverbs 29:25 says, "Fearing people is a dangerous trap, but trusting the Lord means safety."

Growing up, my biggest fear was of people. They posed the biggest threat to my safety, because they could hurt me. But I was only digging a deeper hole for myself, because the more I hid from people, the lonelier and more miserable I was. I created a very painful existence for myself - alone.

God didn't create people to hide from each other. He created us to be in families, communities, churches, friendships. He intended people for relationships. True safety comes from trusting him, not hiding from those he created us to live in fellowship with.

In trying to protect myself from pain, I only hurt myself more. It wasn't until I began to open myself up to the potential for pain by knowing others that I began to heal.

Overcoming the Victim Mindset

Romans 12:3-13 says, "Because of the privilege and authority God has given me, I give each of you this warning: Don't think you are better than you really are. Be honest in your evaluation of yourselves, measuring yourselves by the faith God has given us. Just as our bodies have many parts and each part has a special function, so it is with Christ's body. We are many parts of one body, and we all belong to each other. In his grace, God has given us different gifts for doing certain things well. So if God has given you the ability to prophesy, speak out with as much faith as God has given you. If your gift is serving others, serve them well. If you are a teacher, teach well. If your gift is to encourage others, be encouraging. If it is giving, give generously. If God has given you leadership ability, take the responsibility seriously. And if you have a gift for showing kindness to others, do it gladly. Don't just pretend to love others. Really love them. Hate what is wrong. Hold tightly to what is good. Love each other with genuine affection, and take delight in honoring each other. Never be lazy, but work hard and serve the Lord enthusiastically. Rejoice in our confident hope. Be patient in trouble, and keep on praying. When God's people are in need, be ready to help them. Always be eager to practice hospitality."

One of the first things I had to learn about relationships is **do not be a victim.** The victim mindset will kill love in any relationship. In this current season, God is teaching me in my marriage to not act like a wounded wife. A wounded mindset does not stay in one area. It takes root and spreads in all directions, fast. It will go anywhere you allow it to.

I struggled a lot with feeling like a victim of ignorance in relationships. How could I really make a difference to anyone if no one ever taught me anything? But the problem isn't that no one ever taught me anything about relationship skills. The problem is what I do with what I was given. I now have the resources available to me to learn anything I need to know.

I am not a victim of ignorance, laziness, or fear. I'm not a victim of anger at the people who caused the ignorance. God didn't ask me to know all the answers, but to be committed to learning and growing.

Matthew 25:14-30 says, "Again, the Kingdom of Heaven can be illustrated by the story of a man going on a long trip. He called together his servants and entrusted his money to them while he was gone. He gave five bags of silver to one, two bags of silver to another, and one bag of silver to the last - dividing it in proportion to their abilities. He then left on his trip.

"The servant who received the five bags of silver began to invest the money and earned five more. The servant with two bags of silver also went to work and earned two more. But the servant who received the one bag of silver dug a hole in the ground and hid the master's money.

"After a long time their master returned from his trip and called them to give an account of how they had used his money. The servant to whom he had entrusted the five bags of silver came forward with five more and said, 'Master, you gave me five bags of silver to invest, and I have earned five more.'

"The master was full of praise. 'Well done, my good and faithful servant. You have been faithful in handling this small amount, so now I will give you many more responsibilities. Let's celebrate together!'

"The servant who had received the two bags of silver came forward and said, 'Master, you gave me two bags of silver to invest, and I have earned two more.'

"The master said, 'Well done, my good and faithful servant. You have been faithful in handling this small amount, so now I will give you many more responsibilities. Let's celebrate together!'

"Then the servant with the one bag of silver came and said, 'Master, I knew you were a harsh man, harvesting crops you didn't plant and gathering crops you didn't cultivate. I was afraid I would lose your money, so I hid it in the earth. Look, here is your money back.'

"But the master replied, 'You wicked and lazy servant! If you knew I harvested crops I didn't plant and gathered crops I didn't cultivate, why didn't you deposit my money in the bank? At least I could have gotten some interest on it.'

"Then he ordered, 'Take the money from this servant, and give it to the one with the ten bags of silver. To those who use well what they are given, even more will be given, and they will have an abundance. But from those who do nothing, even what little they have will be taken away. Now throw this useless servant into outer darkness, where there will be weeping and gnashing of teeth.'"

The passage in Romans 12 and this passage in Matthew 25 is all about obedience. Obedience is about being faithful to the responsibilities that God has entrusted me with. Obedience is how my life expresses love for God.

Each person is entrusted with a gift from God. It is not the gift that matters; it is what we do with it that matters. The amount of the gift is not relevant, because the gift is multiplied through obedience.

What does all of this have to do with relationships?

A lot of relationships are stunted and stuck in selfish ambition because of a lack of development of the gifts we've been given. A lot of us are too afraid to step up and lead others or to show kindness or to be seen, because we are more afraid of failure than of not obeying.

Paul says in Romans 12 that we are each a part of Christ's body and that each part has a special function. But if we are claiming to be wounded and victimizing ourselves to the unfairness of our circumstances, how is the body of Christ going to function? It is time to stop allowing our wounds to stunt our growth. Stop allowing our wounds to shut down our gifts. The body of Christ is not a place where wounds should be licked. The body of Christ is a place of healing, empathy, and compassion. The body of Christ is where God who is Love dwells. But healing does not happen through self-pity. Healing happens when we allow the Father's tender hands to touch us. And his tender healing brings out our gifts through our wounded areas. Our hurts can become our strength, when we allow Love Himself to fill our wounds.

For Jesus to be able to save the world, he had to be completely broken first. He had to literally die. There was no way for a resurrection to happen without death. He made it so that in our places of pain, there is always healing for someone else.

2 Corinthians 1:3-7 says, "All praise to God, the Father of our Lord Jesus Christ. God is our merciful Father and the source of all comfort. He comforts us in all our troubles so that we can comfort others. When they are troubled, we will be able to give them the same comfort God has given us. For the more we suffer for Christ, the more God will shower us with his comfort through Christ. Even when we are weighed down with troubles, it is for your comfort and salvation! For when we ourselves are comforted, we will certainly comfort you. Then you can patiently endure the same things we suffer. We are confident that as you share in our sufferings, you will also share in the comfort God gives us."

Earlier in this chapter, I was talking about how a lot of people view God as the cause of their pain. In the parable of the talents (or in this version, the bags of silver), the servant with one bag of silver called his master "a harsh man." He viewed himself as the victim of his master. He was afraid of losing his gift, so he buried it. Ironically, he was the one who not only lost his gift but was thrown out of his master's presence.

Paul, in 2 Corinthians 1, presents us with a different mindset. He names God a "merciful Father and the source of all comfort." Not only is God a good Father who shows us understanding and grace, he went through everything we do as a man on earth so that he could redeem us and adopt us as his own children.

Peter gives an amazing view of these two mindsets and the difference each makes in our lives.

2 Peter 1:3-11 says, "By his divine power, God has given us everything we need for living a godly life. We have received all of this by coming to know him, the one who called us to himself by means of his marvelous glory and excellence. And because of his glory and excellence, he has given us great and precious promises. These are the promises that enable you to share his divine nature and escape the world's corruption caused by human desires.

"In view of all this, make every effort to respond to God's promises. Supplement your faith with a generous provision of moral excellence, and moral excellence with knowledge, and knowledge with self-control, and self-control with patient endurance, and patient endurance with godliness, and godliness with brotherly affection, and brotherly affection with love for everyone.

"The more you grow like this, the more productive and useful you will be in your knowledge of our Lord Jesus Christ. But those who fail to develop in this way are shortsighted or blind, forgetting that they have been cleansed from their old sins.

"So, dear brothers and sisters, work hard to prove that you really are among those God has called and chosen. Do these things, and you will never fall away. Then God will give you a grand entrance into the eternal Kingdom of our Lord and Savior Jesus Christ."

Blaming God and playing the victim reveals shortsightedness or blindness. We have a filter of fear over our eyes, hindering our growth and stopping our effectiveness. It causes us to forget that before we knew God, we were sinners, and our problems are in fact not God's fault at all, but sin's.

The other mindset is fueled by faith in God's promises. It is a knowledge that God will come through, because that is his character. But it goes beyond knowing, to actively living a life that proves you believe that God does what he says. With each outward step of obedience, it solidifies and proves your inward heart of faith. The outward actions express your inner relationship with God.

Imagine the differences with each mindset. Blaming God means that we are also most likely blaming others. But faith in God, regardless of what he's given us, means that we are also choosing to love others.

#1

The first step in overcoming the victim mindset is to forgive. I have mentioned this repeatedly, because it is so important. Forgiveness is a cornerstone of a believer's faith. A believer who refuses to forgive is rendered ineffective, blind, and useless - exactly what Peter described.

#2

The next step is to show kindness instead of taking offense. Offenses happen often. Reasons to be offended are numerous. But offenses taken personally and used as weapons to fight back are an expression of victimization. Releasing the offense and using it as a reason to be kind takes you to the opposite side of the spectrum.

#3

Bind the lie of rejection. I believed I was rejected in relationships, until I forgave the hurt. Then I recognized that rejection is nothing but a lie from the enemy who wants to steal, kill, and destroy and is the father of lies. Rejection is real. Rejection hurts. But staying in a place of rejection when you are called to rise above it hurts you more than it helps you.

These are some practical things I've learned over the past few years.

- Figure out what you're most afraid of and prepare well in that area. Do whatever it takes to make yourself socially acceptable to yourself. Find out what you expect of yourself socially. My struggle is that I disqualify myself before I even try. The root of my struggle is self-hatred.

- Find out what you want other people to do to you and do it to them. What do they do to you that makes you feel loved? What kind of person do you want to be socially? How do you want others to see you?

- Figure out your weak areas and learn how to solve them ahead of time. Become strong in your weak areas, and your self-confidence will grow.

- Find out what you bring to the table. No one really connects in the same way, and that's okay. Just bring what you have to offer.

- I heard someone say once that you are either a fountain or a drain. People gather around fountains.

- Being a fountain takes a lot of wisdom. Jesus promised to be a well of living water in us, so we are not on our own.

- Develop curiosity about others. Make questions your friends. Questions that go beneath the surface. Open-ended questions.
- Don't be shy. Shyness is real, but it can be overcome through effort and learning. Shyness is never helpful.
- Use eye contact.
- Pray for friends. God cares about your social life.
- Find friends who enjoy the same things you do. Common interests make connection easier.
- Find out others' love languages and plan activities/do things that make them feel loved. Don't love how you want to be loved. Don't love out of a desire for approval.
- Give unselfishly.
- Use humor as a skill to make others feel comfortable and relaxed.
- Don't be a pushover. Push back and argue if needed. There are healthy and unhealthy ways of doing this. Talk about things that bother you.
- Don't gossip.
- Don't manipulate.
- Learn how to communicate well.

There are many videos to watch on YouTube and there are many books to read to learn people skills.

What is in your hand today that you can use to love someone with?

Exercises

#1 Reveal

What am I feeling right now?

Why am I feeling this way?

What lies am I believing?

Where do the lies come from?

What am I allowing to control my mind?

What shuts me down?

What causes me to stop dreaming?

What is my biggest fear?

#2 Release

This step is all about creating awareness. When you have lived for a long time with habits of thinking a certain way, it requires a commitment to daily train yourself to think differently-not an easy task. Catch yourself in the act of believing a lie. Don't let the lie go. It's easy to slip, especially in the beginning. The beginning is the hardest.

Find the Scripture verses that speak to the lies in your head. I have often turned on audio Scriptures when Satan was fighting to shut my mouth. Not today, Satan!

Speak those verses out loud. The louder, the better. I remember many car drives when I would use the time to really get the words out with volume. Spoken words shift the atmosphere drastically. Satan hears what you say. Say it as though you believe it! Take authority over your mind.

Journal section:

Bible verses:

#3 Replace

Once you have become honest about your struggles, and you are working to create awareness where you need to change your belief systems, you need to replace the lies with the truth.

This is a constant process. Your brain has literal grooves in it from thinking the same way for so long. It takes time and repetition to change it, to create new grooves. This is where the bigger tests happen.

Replacing the lies with the truth happens when you constantly, with awareness and intention, tell yourself something different. It won't happen by accident. It won't happen by itself. It takes work. Especially when you are struggling with a lie, that is when you need to tell yourself the truth.

Journal section:

#4 Forgive

Forgiveness is often pure choice. It rarely has anything to do with feelings. In fact, you may still feel anger and hatred. But in the middle of feeling angry and hateful, the choice to forgive has the power to break those chains. Only Jesus has the power to help you to choose forgiveness through heated emotions.

Journal section:

Who do I need to forgive?

For what do I need to forgive?

ACKNOWLEDGEMENTS

I would like to thank Judith Martin for pouring hours into teaching me and for buying me so many coffees. You were the inspiration behind so much of this content. I can't even express how much I appreciate everything you have done for me. I certainly would never have written this book without you. Thank you for believing in me.

I would like to thank Gloria Volcov for her contribution. I have seen the change in you as you grew in your faith, even though we don't live in the same state. I pray for God to use your gift of writing to touch hearts far and wide. You have a beautiful heart.

I would like to thank my son, Liam. You are only one year old, and you spent all those hours with me, while I was working on this project. As I am writing this, you keep trying to hit my keyboard. Thank you for hanging out with me and having so much patience with me while I was working.

I would like to thank my husband, Mike. Thank you for spending so much time listening to me talk about this project. You are my strongest supporter. I couldn't have done this without you. Thank you for helping me through all the spiritual turbulence during this project. Our marriage has become stronger through this time.

I would like to thank my heavenly Father, God. You have been so patient with me as I have stumbled and fought my way through this growing process. You are so kind. You were always present to give me words as I wrote. You led me through this whole project. Your hand is all over it. Thank You, Lord. I would not be writing this book without you. I stand in awe of your work in my life. I love You.

RESOURCES

These are a few of my favorite books that I recommend.

Winning the War in Your Mind by Craig Groeschel

The Social Skills Guidebook: Manage Shyness, Improve Your Conversations, and Make Friends, Without Giving Up Who You Are by Chris MacLeod

The Wise Wife Blueprint: Biblical Solutions for Finding Joy in Any Marriage by Natasha Drisdelle

Lioness Arising: Wake Up and Change Your World by Lisa Bevere

The Lost Art of True Beauty: The Set-Apart Girl's Guide to Feminine Grace by Leslie Ludy

Instruments in the Redeemer's Hands: People in Need of Change Helping People in Need of Change by Paul David Tripp

Becoming Free Indeed: My Story of Disentangling Faith from Fear by Jinger Vuolo